Restating the State?

Blackwell
Publishing

PQ

Restating the State?

Edited by

Andrew Gamble and Tony Wright

Blackwell Publishing
In association with *The Political Quarterly*

Set in 9.5/11pt Palatino by Anne Joshua & Associates, Oxford
Printed and bound in the United Kingdom by Cambrian Printers Ltd, Aberystwyth
For further information on Blackwell Publishing, visit our website:
www.blackwellpublishing.com

Contents

Notes on Contributors

Norman Barry is Professor of Social and Political Theory at the University of Buckingham.

Colin Crouch is Professor of Sociology at the European University Institute, Florence; from January 2005 he will be Chair of the Institute of Governance and Public Management at the Warwick Business School.

Andrew Gamble is Professor of Politics at the University of Sheffield and joint editor of *The Political Quarterly*; his most recent book is *Between Europe and America: The Future of British Politics* (Palgrave, 2003).

Colin Hay is Professor of Political Analysis and Head of the Department of Political Science and International Studies at the University of Birmingham.

John Kay is Visiting Professor, London School of Economics.

Charles Leadbeater is a research associate of the think tank Demos and the Design Council.

David Marquand is Former Principal of Mansfield College, Oxford, and Visiting Fellow, Department of Politics and International Relations, Oxford University.

B. Guy Peters is Maurice Falk Professor of American Government at the University of Pittsburgh.

Raymond Plant has been a Labour Member of the House of Lords since 1992 and is Professor of Jurisprudence and Political Philosophy at King's College Law School, London University.

Gerry Stoker is Professor of Politics, Institute for Political and Economic Governance and School of the Social Sciences at the University of Manchester.

Hilary Wainwright is editor of *Red Pepper* magazine, Research Director of the New Politics project of the Transnational Institute, and author of several books including most recently *Reclaim the State: Experiments in Popular Democracy* (Verso, 2003).

David Walker is editor of *Public*, the *Guardian*'s monthly magazine for executives across the public sector.

Tony Wright is the Member of Parliament for Cannock Chase, chair of the Public Administration Select Committee, and joint editor of *The Political Quarterly*; his most recent book is *British Politics: A Very Short Introduction* (OUP, 2003).

Introduction

ANDREW GAMBLE and TONY WRIGHT

IN HIS essay *The End of Laissez-faire*, first published in 1926, Keynes distinguished between the agenda and the non-agenda of government. 'The important thing for government', he wrote, 'is not to do things which individuals are doing already, and to do them a little better or a little worse; but to do those things which at present are not done at all.'[1] Keynes was writing near the beginning of the great expansion in both the scope and scale of the state which became the hallmark of a certain kind of social democracy and progressive politics. Almost eighty years on, what does Keynes's distinction mean today? How have the agenda and the non-agenda of government shifted, and how might they shift further in the future?

The two world wars moved the scale of the state in Britain decisively upwards. From less than 8 per cent of GDP before 1914, the state accounted for over 20 per cent in the 1920s and 1930s, and this rose again to 40 per cent after 1945. It has fluctuated around this level ever since. Currently it stands at 42 per cent. The state has not expanded very much, but neither has it contracted. Despite the rhetoric of 'rolling back the state' in the Thatcher years, and New Right dreams of a return to the minimal state of Victorian times, the actual size of the state has remained remarkably constant. It proved much easier to return public utilities from state ownership to private ownership than it did to make real inroads into the core spending programmes of the modern state, and therefore to reduce the overall tax burden.

However, this apparent constancy in the size of the state disguises some major changes in the way the state is now organised and run. The social democratic state that was established in Britain after 1945 has been subjected to major challenges in the last thirty years by neo-liberal ideas and policies which have caused a significant rethinking of the nature of the state, its objectives and its capacities, on both right and left. New doctrines for managing the state, new conceptions of the state and new ideas for organising the delivery of public services have abounded: new public management, the enabling state, the hollowing out of the state, the competition state, the market state and public–private partnerships are just a few of these. This book explores this recent experience, and asks: how should we now understand the state and what choices lie before us?

Socialists have often been ambivalent about the state. Many nineteenth century socialists regarded the state as the arm of property and capital, and talked of either overthrowing it, or of building a new form of state parallel to the existing one, based on decentralised, local, accountable associations. In either case the existing state was set to wither away. Only with the gradual

© The Political Quarterly Publishing Co. Ltd. 2004
Published by Blackwell Publishing Ltd, 9600 Garsington Road, Oxford OX4 2DQ, UK and 350 Main Street, Malden, MA 02148, USA

spread of representative institutions and a democratic franchise did the arguments for taking control of the state and using it for socialist and progressive aims begin to gain ground. In the twentieth century many socialists became enthusiastic statists, persuaded that the state could be used to deliver universal and uniform policies for an entire national community. Social democratic priorities could be imposed through the collective machinery of the state. Some on the left, such as the guild socialists, remained sceptical ('In the State of today', wrote GDH Cole in his *Self-Government in Industry* (1917), 'in which democratic control through Parliament is little better than a farce, the Collectivist State would be the Earthly Paradise of bureaucracy'); but these were minority traditions.

The building of the twentieth century welfare state in Britain and elsewhere reached its zenith in the postwar decades. Reacting against the pervasive failure of markets and the classical liberal prescriptions of sound money, free trade and *laissez-faire*, the new consensus across right and left emphasised planning, state initiative, universalism, and common standards for all citizens. But there were always critics on the right who feared the rise of a bureaucratic state which would threaten liberty, as well as critics on the left who charged that this bureaucratic state had more to do with shoring up, stabilising and modernising capitalism than with inaugurating genuine equality and self-government. In the 1970s the interruption to postwar economic growth, and the emergence of new threats and challenges, created not only a fiscal crisis but a crisis about the affordability and desirability of the welfare state.

In retrospect, the difficulties of the 1970s, although exaggerated at the time, did represent a turning point in British policy. Whereas some other European states moved to extend and deepen their welfare states, Britain failed to create the institutions and partnerships that were needed to sustain further development and reform of its welfare state, and this opened the door to the radical critique of assorted neo-liberals and neo-conservatives grouped under the political leadership of Margaret Thatcher. The dismantling of what remained of Britain's corporatist experiment, the privatisation of state enterprises, a succession of laws to remove trade union legal privileges, together with a tough economic policy that saw unemployment rise to over 3 million, all followed.

What was also noticeable, not least to many of the ideologues of the Thatcher Revolution, was that the radicalism of the government appeared to ebb the closer it approached the central problem, the core programmes of the welfare state. Ignominious retreats over student fees and school vouchers were early portents. Although the Thatcher government had proclaimed in its 1980 White Paper that 'public expenditure is at the heart of our current difficulties', it had failed to reduce the proportion of public spending in GDP by 1990 when Margaret Thatcher left office. The Major government fared little better. What the Thatcher government did attempt to do (and this was continued in a more systematic manner under John Major) was to try to

2

reform the way the public sector operated. It embraced enthusiastically the doctrines of the new public management, splitting the purchaser from the supplier, creating a myriad of new agencies charged with running public services, dismantling the hierarchical bureaucratic structures which had characterised the big government departments, and instituting the regime of targets and performance indicators, perpetual monitoring, and the rise of the audit society.

The Thatcher government was supposed to be a great privatising government, and in respect of public utilities and of council houses this was true. But in the sphere of public services the government privatised very little. It introduced more private companies into the provision of services, but the core funding remained resolutely state funding. It also introduced internal markets into many parts of the public services, in the hope that by simulating conditions in the private sector both competition and efficiency would be increased. Under these reforms power was shifted away from civil servants and away from the professions to a new breed of managers. The professions were generally viewed with suspicion by Conservative ministers as the source of vested interests, obstacles to change, and inefficient and self-serving working practices.

By the end of eighteen years in government the Conservatives' policy had clearly failed. They had at best kept the lid on public spending, failing to produce the dramatic scaling down of government which the ideologues of the New Right had hoped for, by creating free markets in health care and education, and making individuals responsible for providing for themselves. At the same time they had also failed to gain public confidence in the quality of the public services, which were widely regarded by 1997 as seriously under-funded and producing low quality outcomes, despite all the reforms which the new public management had introduced into the way in that they were run.

New Labour offered a change of direction, but not in all respects. It did not discard the new techniques and institutions which had been created under the Conservatives to run the state. Many of them, like the Private Finance Initiative (PFI), it embraced with enthusiasm and carried much further. The main change it initiated, after two years of following the Conservatives' own spending plans in order to establish its credibility with the financial markets, was to announce spending plans that projected substantially increased budgets for all the core welfare programmes for first three and then five years ahead.[2] This began one of the largest sustained increases in the size of the British welfare state since the 1940s, and one that had consistently eluded Labour governments in the 1960s and 1970s, which had tended to announce large increases in public spending when they entered office, much of which had later to be clawed back in the ensuing financial crises.

The approach of new Labour has been cautious and incremental, but over time, and particularly if Labour is re-elected for a third term, the cumulative effect of its policies will be significant. Labour has been much less successful in pushing through the reforms it says are essential if the extra funding is not to be wasted. The bruising battles over foundation hospitals and variable fees for universities are two examples where the government has sought to encourage greater diversity and local self-government in the management of public services, seeking to push up standards and encourage greater efficiency; but its opponents have charged that Labour's reforms threaten to undermine the core principles of uniformity and universalism of provision enshrined in the postwar welfare state, and open the door to creeping privatisation.

The issues that the history of the last twenty-five years raise for the role of the state are profound. We appear to have reached a kind of crossroads. There is a *de facto* consensus on the size of the state between the main parties, as indeed there was in the 1950s, but this conceals, as it did then, a deeper disagreement about the role and purpose of the state. Some see the present period as one in which with the establishment since the mid-1990s of a reasonably successful political economy—high employment, low inflation and moderate growth—Britain has settled for a liberal rather than a social democratic welfare regime, with the choice between the parties lying between modest redistribution and modest tax cuts.

A more persuasive view is that Britain's political economy remains a hybrid and reflects an enduring political stalemate about the purposes and role of the state. Public spending is either too low or too high. Some public services remain universal and free at the point of need; others are highly selective and targeted, often skewed in favour of higher income groups. The choice between a substantial expansion of the state to something closer to European standards, or a substantial contraction to something close to the United States, is unresolved. What complicates the choice is that we live in an era in which the reach of the state continues to expand, yet faith in the state to deliver is contracting. The state is expected to do more and more, to solve an extraordinary array of problems, but the citizens at the same time seem to have less and less faith in its ability to do so. Even when presented with evidence that the state has delivered, this tends to be discounted, because expectations run ahead of performance. This presents problems for those who wish the state to disengage from running the public services and from intervening in the economy or society, as well as for those who wish the state to do more. Establishing trust in an organisation which has grown so large and complex, in which lines of accountability are so hard to trace or understand, and in which forms of knowledge are so difficult to evaluate, poses huge problems. But policies bent on the serious dismantling of the state have not won public support.

The future role of the state will depend on how a number of key issues are resolved. All involve intractable dilemmas. The first of these is public value. Labour has sought to restore the idea of the public good of publicly funded services, in a bid to bring fresh legitimacy to the idea of active government and comprehensive public services as the backbone of national community. It has redefined the old idea of a national minimum wage, and consolidated universal programmes and even introduced some new ones, like the child trust fund.[3] It has gone some way to rebuilding confidence in the public services, but this remains vulnerable to all those pressures which are undermining a sense of public ethos, shrinking the public domain and eroding support for universal programmes. Some of these pressures are created by the means chosen to deliver higher standards in public services, such as targets and PFI. There is a constant struggle between the need to raise standards and to maintain the morale and support of those working in the public services. The key question is whether universal programmes in health, education and social security belong today to the agenda or non-agenda of government in Keynes's sense. The social democratic argument is that without the state these things would not be done at all; the neo-liberal argument is that they would all be better done through free markets and individual choice.

The second issue is autonomy, and is closely related to the first. A new definition of public value has to accommodate ways of allowing individuals to choose and exercise more control. Whether the state can be reformed so as to decentralise decision making and re-energise civil society, without sacrificing the sense of national community which the old welfare state provided, is still uncertain. Evidence of declining support for collective welfare and redistribution, and the resistance in practice (if not always in opinion polls) to higher taxes, makes a slow incremental slide towards a much more residual welfare regime entirely plausible. Something similar occurred in the 1980s after all. The old command state cannot be resurrected, although it did have some virtues.[4] The challenge is rather different—whether new forms of self-government in local communities and in the public services themselves can be established which can offer an alternative to the command model, to the managerial model, and to the market model alike.

A third issue is citizenship, which is tied up with the vexed issues of the definition of national community in an increasingly interdependent and mobile world. Who the state represents, to whom it has obligations, and to whom it is accountable have always been key questions in politics. Issues of migration and of membership of regional associations like the European Union raise these issues starkly for Britain. A closed national community guaranteeing very high levels of welfare and public services to its citizens is one socialist model, but not an appealing one. Expanding as well as deepening citizenship has always been part of progressive politics, but is particularly hard to sustain in the face of nationalist and xenophobic pressures. Solidarity is one of the central social democratic values that an active state seeks to nurture and strengthen, but international solidarity is always vulnerable to the claims of national security. Finding a bridge between these two is one of the hardest tasks in democratic politics.[5]

Finally, there is the issue of well-being. After a period in which the prevailing argument has been that many matters in which the state took an interest are better left to markets, there are signs of a swing back to the need to restore the idea of the public and the public domain.[6] New agendas for the state and other public bodies are emerging, many of them concerned with the idea of well-being, which goes far beyond questions of material need to questions of the quality of work and quality of life, the balance between work and other activities, gender roles, the capacities individuals need to live a full human life, poverty and social exclusion. Many of these are values beyond the market and cannot be reduced to a financial calculus, but instead require clear limits to be established to the role of markets in our society. Here as elsewhere the state cannot impose, only at best enable, and the enabling is often best done not by state agencies themselves but by bodies in civil society. But the state is still needed to set the framework, and provide the incentives, and to help reinforce a particular definition of the public good and the public interest. That is what the state exists for, and it is a function only the state can perform. Whether the ideal is a neo-liberal free market society with only a minimal state, or a social democratic society with an active and enabling state, there is still the need for a state to underpin and sustain that society, to decide what matters can be left to individuals, and what matters the state itself needs to undertake.

We have clearly come a long way since R. H. Tawney could describe the state simply as a 'serviceable drudge'.[7] This description was perhaps effective enough in providing social democratic reassurance about the mundane operation of an expanded state against the nightmare warnings of Hayek and others. Yet it is no longer adequate as an analysis of the state, not least because it deliberately closes down issues that we now want to open up. The old taken-for-granted view of the state is precisely what needs to be examined, not because the functions of the state are less necessary but because there is now much more attention to the way in which these functions are performed. The state may indeed be a drudge, but it is the nature of this drudgery that is now under acute examination.

It was examined recently by Gordon Brown in an important and much-noticed lecture[8] described in the *Financial Times* as 'a formidable account of modern social democracy'. At the heart of his argument was the shifting relationship between state and market, in contrast to 'the old sterile and debilitating conflicts of the past'. Both markets and the state have to be made to work better, if the public interest is to be advanced. This means a robust competition policy to ensure that markets function properly, but it also means that 'we renegotiate the relationship between markets and government'. Sometimes this will mean extending the role of markets; at other times (as in health) understanding where markets have inherent deficiencies so that the state has to provide. This was offered as an approach that goes beyond the old categories of left and right by introducing a test of public interest against which both markets and state have to be judged.

This has radical implications. It means recognising that 'enhancing markets will mean reducing government'. But it also means recognising where markets fail, or are inappropriate. However, where the argument really gets interesting, and the challenge for progressives becomes sharpest, is in relation to areas where the market is judged inappropriate but where traditional state models of service organisation and delivery do not work well either. Here Gordon Brown could not be clearer: 'It is only by developing decentralised non market models for public provision that respond to people's needs, extend choice and are equitable and efficient that we will show to those who assert that whatever the market failure the state failure will always be greater that a publicly funded and provided service can deliver efficiency, equity and be responsive to the consumer'. Equity need not mean uniformity, nor need diversity mean inequality. Although he eschews the language of the third way, this reconciliation of opposites sits at its centre.

In this version, though, it acquires a much sharper intellectual edge. This does not dissolve its difficulties (at what point does diversity conflict with equity? how can choice be offered by a monopoly provider?), but at least it opens up arguments that matter. It is not enough for the left to 'defend' the state against the market. The task now is to develop versions of the state that show that non-market provision can be efficient and responsive to the needs of users. It is a bogus kind of public service ethos that puts the interests of service providers before those of service users, just as it should be unacceptable to settle for the equity of universal mediocrity. These are not abstract considerations. The social democratic model, in its revised version, is on trial. If it is seen to fail, the terms of political trade will sooner or later turn against it.

It is the left's job to show that the state, its chosen instrument for equity and efficiency on a range of key fronts, can actually work. This political imperative should have made it a relentless innovator as far as public services are concerned, instead of a conservative defender of every available status quo. It should not have come as a revelation to it that outcomes, not inputs, are what matter, or that public services are not run for the benefit of those who provide them. The fact that the Blair government has recognised that the state must look different as a result of its period of government should be counted an advance, not a retreat (let alone a betrayal).

But how different? This is where the difficulties start, and where the real arguments have to engage. Gordon Brown has correctly identified the territory, but how this territory is to be negotiated remains the crucial challenge. The arguments about foundation hospitals and specialist schools, where diversity as a stimulus to excellence collides with equity as a claim to common provision, test the inherent tensions. So too does the issue of choice, which on one view empowers users and on another view merely enables some to jump the queue. Unless we are content to deny such tensions, which would be foolish, the task is how to reconcile them in relation to particular areas. It becomes a matter of boundaries and balances. This is where the hard thinking now needs to be done.

Such thinking should extend more widely too. It is a crucial moment in the permanent debate between localism and centralism. If a better balance is to be struck, then a 'new' localism has to become more than a defence of existing models of local government and must genuinely think about how effective accountabilities can be developed at the local level. Similarly, if the crushing weight of centrally imposed targets and inspections is to be lifted from public bodies of all kinds, it has to be because those who run such bodies accept the requirements of high performance and embrace a version of professionalism that incorporates a proper accountability. This means attention to issues of management and leadership.

The boundaries of state and market are in flux, and in many areas state and market now inhabit the same territory. How these boundaries are policed and regulated becomes a fundamental issue, if the test of public interest is to be the primary consideration. In many respects the issue is not whether the state should be bigger or smaller, but how it can be smarter. For too long it has been those on the political right who have been preoccupied with rethinking the state. This is curious, in view of the centrality of the state to the left. It is an omission that now needs to be remedied.

We hope that the chapters that follow contribute to this task. What they have in common is an impatience with old categories and dichotomies, and a desire to open up new conceptual (and practical) territory. There is not a common agenda, but there is a shared sense of the need to go beyond traditional thinking about the state if its contemporary role is to be adequately identified. It is not that such thinking, and the arguments associated with it, have ceased to matter, but that they are framed in different ways. There is, for example, less attention to defending the old boundaries of market and state and more to exploring how public value can be augmented by new relationships between market and state, and what role the state has in nourishing a wider public realm.

In all the contributions here there is a sense of new thinking, and new applications of such thinking, being required. Thus Norman Barry marshals the classical case for a minimal state, but concludes that state growth is seemingly ineluctable and so the question becomes 'how do we get the public goods, which are essential for social cooperation, without unintentionally producing an extensive state?' Raymond Plant also carefully examines the neo-liberal account of the state, which he regards as powerful and coherent, but suggests that its 'fatal weakness' turns on the claims it makes about the market order with which it is inextricably linked. Colin Hay notes a 'poverty of contemporary state theory' among social scientists, and discusses the limitations of such theory as does exist, thereby also making the case for new thinking about the nature of the modern state.

Other contributors want to tease out, and argue for, the public policy implications of what they say about the state. David Marquand laments the 'ingrained *étatisme*' of the social democratic tradition, and especially of its British version, and argues for a kind of state that nourishes a public realm rather than stifles it. By contrast, David Walker's case is that the British have not been *étatiste* enough, and this 'absence of state' has to be remedied by its robust assertion if policy failures are to be avoided. John Kay repudiates the old boundary lines of state and market in favour of a 'disciplined pluralism' that nourishes flexibility and innovation through a variety of hybrid structures. This approach is also reflected in Charles Leadbeater's 'variable geometry public sector', in which the state promotes organisational diversity and stimulates initiative in others.

The focus on diversity is shared by Colin Crouch, requiring the state to be an energetic and creative actor in relation to 'the rich and complex mixes of economic governance that are appearing'. In terms of political governance, Gerry Stoker argues for a 'more differentiated local state system' as the appropriate response to the complex demands made of it. However, Guy Peters notes an emerging trend towards some 'recentring of the state' as an attempt to recover coherent governing capacity. Finally, Hilary Wainwright explores the principles and practices of a 'democratic public administration' which also goes beyond the old dichotomies of state and market into a 'third dimension' of governing possibilities.

This is rich and varied fare. There is a dissatisfaction with the limitations of traditional 'state versus market' arguments and an exploration of the terrain that is opened up once such limitations are transcended. This does not meant that a role for the state in resisting inappropriate encroachments by the market is less necessary (far from it), but it does not mean a more creative role for the state than that implied by a conventional 'public goods' approach to state action. It may even presage a break from the cyclical oscillations that have long characterised thinking about the state: the minimal state ascendancy of *laissez-faire* doctrines up to the last quarter of the nineteenth century, the age of collectivism that then established itself for nearly a century thereafter, and the neo-liberal resurgence from the 1970s. If so, this would indeed be an important moment in the restating of the state.

Notes

1 J. M. Keynes, *The End of Laissez-Faire*, London, Hogarth Press, 1926.
2 For example, the 2002 plans aimed to raise education spending to £69 billion per annum in 2008 (from £36 billion in 1997) and health spending to £106 billion per annum (from £41 billion in 1997).
3 Gavin Kelly, Andrew Gamble and Will Paxton 'Stakeholding and individual ownership accounts', in K. Dowding, J. De Wispelaere and S. White, eds, *The Ethics of Stakeholding*, London, Palgrave Macmillan, 2003, pp. 42–64.
4 Richard Sennett, *Respect: The Formation of Character in an Age of Inequality*, London, Penguin 2004.
5 Sarah Spencer, ed., *The Politics of Managed Migration*, Oxford, Blackwell, 2003.

6 David Marquand, *Decline of the Public*, Cambridge, Polity, 2003.
7 R. H. Tawney, 'Social democracy in Britain' (1949), in R. Hinden, ed., *The Radical Tradition*, Penguin, 1966.
8 Gordon Brown, 'State and market: towards a public interest test', *The Political Quarterly*, vol. 74, no. 3, July–September 2003.

The Rationale of the Minimal State

NORMAN BARRY

WITH perhaps the exception of Robert Nozick's *Anarchy, State and Utopia*, the rationale of the minimalist state usually derives, negatively, from an economic critique of the extensive state. For despite the collapse of communism and the move towards free markets throughout the world we still live in significantly statist societies. Most Western capitalist countries have large public sectors, many of which spend up to 50% of Gross Domestic Product; America and Japan spend about 35%, and the United Kingdom now spends 42%, expenditure having been as low as 37% in the 1980s. Extensive privatisation has seen the state withdraw from the economy in goods and services but it is still a huge player in welfare, education and health. Sometimes it is a monopoly supplier in these fields but most states allow competition with private agencies. Furthermore, the rise of international organisations, such as the European Union, has introduced a modified statism in the form of heavy regulation rather than old-fashioned nationalisation.

The process of withdrawal of the state from civil society has been, not surprisingly, most enthusiastically greeted by former communist regimes. The prime example is Estonia, which has embraced a dominant market sector and completely free trade, and is about to lower its flat tax from 26% to 20%.[1] Its rapid move towards marketisation has been achieved without the crime that almost ruined Russia's move towards capitalism.

The persistence of the state in conventional capitalist economies has elicited sustained criticism from free market economists and classical liberal or libertarian political philosophers. The critics are either natural rights theorists if they are philosophers or utilitarians if they are economists. The former are concerned with morality, the latter with efficiency. The latter take a realistic view of human nature and assume that all agents are utility maximisers, concerned almost exclusively with their own well-being. When people leave the private market and work for the state they do not miraculously shed their egoistic motivations and become imbued with altruism. They may not directly pursue profit but there are other ways in the state sector of maxising utility in a self-interested manner. The difference between the private market and the state is that the former has corrective mechanisms which automatically impel the self-interested person towards the public good. Adam Smith's famous comment is still pertinent today: the person 'intends only his own gain and . . . he is led by an invisible hand to promote an end which was no part of his intention . . . *I have never known much good done by those who affect to trade for the public good*' (my emphasis).[2] To assume otherwise is sentimentality, the bane of modern thinking.

© The Political Quarterly Publishing Co. Ltd. 2004
Published by Blackwell Publishing Ltd, 9600 Garsington Road, Oxford OX4 2DQ, UK and 350 Main Street, Malden, MA 02148, USA   11

Anti-statism has a long history. The great French *laissez-faire* economist Frederic Bastiat put the position succinctly: 'The state is that fictitious institution by which everybody tries to live at the expense of everybody else.'[3] Although his criticism of the state is often understood in efficiency terms, it was actually founded on natural law: the compulsory state is not morally entitled to go beyond what every private person is legitimately entitled to do; that is, defend his person and property against an aggressor. But, in Bastiat's view, the state had ceased to become solely concerned with protection and had become the aggressor itself.

Although his aphorism is a good start, it is not absolutely clear what he meant by 'fictitious'. After all, the state's tax and regulatory powers are quite visible and obviously tangible. It is true that apologists for the state sometimes imply that its activity is not costly for the non-rich; but everybody is aware that state education and health have to be paid for by all taxpayers' money. Perhaps the minimal statist is refuting the communitarian claim that collectively supplied goods and services could not be provided privately and are somehow 'shared'. If they were subject to competition, that would deplete our common membership of society.

Furthermore, Bastiat and other minimal statists are individualists. There is no such thing as an organic state; its aggressive actions are performed by real persons. Minimal statists are certainly ontological individualists. Nevertheless, they adhere to a kind of methodological collectivism: the state has emerged as a powerful institution which does appear to have a will of its own. Although it might have begun with force and aggression, in its modern guise it does seem to march on extensively irrespective of governing parties. It is its ineluctable progress in Western democracies towards the collectivisation of vast areas of hitherto private life that has bothered classical liberals.

Why do we have a state?

Nobody doubts the necessity for law. Certain contingent, but also necessary, features of the human condition imply that all societies need law: limited altruism and our common vulnerability mean that there must be prohibitions against violence, permanent scarcity means that we need laws of property (either public or private), and ignorance of other people's actions necessitates that we need rules as guidelines.[4] One suspects that crime, tort and contract law all find their source in these universal characteristics of humanity. But why the state? Does it not claim a monopoly in protection which could be provided privately? The state was a relative latecomer in European history but there was always law in its predecessor, the Christian Commonwealth. Anthropologists have given vivid accounts of stateless societies. However, the modern world has seen the progressive replacement of the common law, which developed spontaneously without the state, by statute and informal rules of coordination by strict regulation. The modern state in many countries is characterised by sovereignty.

The most sophisticated rationale for state activity derives from the economic theory of public goods. Although we all gain from social cooperation, minimal statists say that it is the perversion of this quite respectable theory that has led to the rise of the state. The big state has not come from communism but from market theory itself. Market economists believe that efficiency is brought about by free exchange between individuals and firms. This assures that only wanted goods are produced (a market derives from choice) and they are produced efficiently because of the free market in capital and labour: they are allocated to their most productive uses. One can see this from the queues, shortages and black markets under communism. Erstwhile socialists now accept this and have even invented an etiolated surrogate of this called market socialism (which largely fails because of the absence of extensive private property and capital markets).

Proper market exchange will always make every one better off: the outcome of exchange is said to be Pareto efficient if there is no putative change which makes no one worse off and at least one person better off. Involuntary public ownership will make many worse off and therefore is not Pareto efficient. There is no value judgement involved in these claims; they are part of the science of wealth creation.

However, there is such a thing as market failure.[5] It has been known since Adam Smith and David Hume that free exchange for technical, but immensely important practical, reasons cannot supply public goods. They are wanted goods which it is in no one market trader's or entrepreneur's interests to supply. Since they cannot be priced he cannot make a profit from them. A public good has two features: it is non-rival in consumption and non-payers cannot be excluded from its enjoyment. It is not like a bar of chocolate which can only be consumed by its owner; once eaten there is nothing left for others. This is not true of defence or clean air. Furthermore, once a public good like defence is provided, non-payers still get its protection, so there is a temptation for everybody to become free riders. These facts mean that nobody will supply the wanted good or service, so the market is not Pareto efficient.

For sound free market reasons, then, the state can make improvements on the market without the resort to value judgements or contentious organic theories. The state can also correct *externalities*, which have the same logic as public goods. Somebody's actions may adversely affect third parties: for example, a factory owner emitting obnoxious fumes from his works. The costs do not appear in his calculus. If very large numbers are affected that might make it impossible to reach a solution by private methods, such as suing for tort. If such transaction costs are too high there is a role for the state. Once again, no value judgement is involved.

It is to be noted that many of the things that are called public goods are not genuine public goods, in the technical sense. Education and health can, and are, subject to the price mechanism. The statists' demand that they be provided publicly cannot derive from efficiency reasons. The stimulus of competition is absent from state suppliers of these services; they will not

respond to demand and will behave like any monopolist in the free market—
they reduce output and raise price (tax).

The advance of the state

Those who believe in a big state do not always use overtly moral arguments to
justify public supply of goods and services but stretch market failure almost
to breaking point. They say, for example, that certain conditions have to be
met for the market to be truly efficient. There are deficiencies in knowledge
which mean that consumers can be exploited by suppliers. In medicine, for
example, asymmetric information between doctor and patient means that the
latter may be compelled to buy treatment he doesn't really need. Again there
could be moral hazard in the insurance market. Once people have paid their
premiums they have every incentive to over-consume. Reasons such as these
are used to explain the vast expenditure on health care in the United States
(14% of GDP). However, minimal statists argue plausibly that competition
amongst insurance companies, and close monitoring of doctors, will keep
health costs down. Furthermore, in a free society it is simply immoral, as well
as inefficient, to make everyone dependent on the monopoly state's supply.
Anyway, empirically, the increase in medical costs in the United States has
come about through the introduction of state supply via Medicare, for the
elderly, and Medicaid, for the poor, in 1965.

The medical example is worth exploring further. It is a paradox of the state
that the vast increase in tax-financed services has not always been in services
that people want. The United Kingdom spends comparatively little on health
(even with recent increased spending it is only approaching 8% of GDP). This
is undoubtedly less than would be spent if tax money were returned to
citizens and they could choose privately. The modern, democratic welfare
state is not efficient at transmitting people's wants. Although people can go
private this means that they are paying twice. In France and Germany health
care is not, in the main, tax financed but is paid for by a complex and
compulsory insurance system. This, of course, means that employers in
France and Germany have high non-wage labour costs but at least consumers
are better satisfied. Even in Italy, whose national health system is not unlike
that in the United Kingdom, private treatment is tax deductible. Equally
important is the fact that British patients effectively face a monopoly supplier
while there is genuine competition in France and Germany. The National
Health Service employs well over a million people, all centrally controlled,
and this gives employees effective bargaining power. But it is also the case
that qualified and efficient personnel in state supplied health and education
do not get the high incomes they could earn in private markets.

The health example fits neatly into another feature of public spending.
People's taxes have to pay for public spending; there is no cornucopia for the
state to draw on. What we pay for in taxes we get back in public services
through a process known as 'churning'.[6] Can we guarantee that there is any

improvement in their quality through the agency of the state? Hardly. It is unlikely that public officials could make efficiency improvements in a heavily unionised public sector. The only rationale for state activity in these areas is the belief that people are too myopic to see where their true interests lie. They have too-high time preferences (they would rather spend today than save for the future) to be concerned about their health, their children's education or to save for their old age. This is simple paternalism and has nothing to do with the original aims of welfare.

There is another public policy which threatens to be, in the long term, even more important than health: I refer to pensions, particularly state pensions.[7] To minimal statists the involvement of the state here is certain to involve both inefficiency and injustice. How much we save for our old age should be a personal decision, determined by our time preferences (how much we value the future). Britain's involvement began in 1908 when the Liberal government first introduced retirement pensions, as a straight welfare measure, unconnected with social insurance. Now almost every liberal democratic country has them (America introduced them in 1935), and they are often linked to lifetime earnings. They are not simple welfare payments but acts of redistribution, normally from the young to the old under what are called 'pay as you go' (PAYG) schemes.

Since state pensions are rarely funded properly their survival depends crucially on two variables, longevity and the birth rate. With advanced medical technology people are living longer (and retiring earlier) and, in Western Europe especially, the birth rate is falling alarmingly. Statists claim that PAYG involves a kind of 'contract between the generations' in which there is an implicit promise by the young to pay for the elderly on the understanding that they will be so generously treated when they retire. But increased longevity and reduced numbers of workers means that such 'agreements' cannot be honoured. Furthermore, when reform comes, as it must do one day, it means that at least one generation will be burdened with the cost of maintaining the present generation of elderly while saving for their own retirement in funded schemes. This is also injustice, as is the phenomenon in America of an implicit discrimination against blacks: they die younger than whites and so receive less Social Security.

The United Kingdom is slightly better off since now around half the population draws pensions from savings which are invested in the stock market. It is an established fact that the return on private investment exceeds the return from tax contributions. In Europe, less than 10% of the population invest privately for their old age and, in contrast to their health arrangements, most people depend on tax-funded, earnings-linked and very expensive retirement payments. France, Germany and Italy (the last two especially) face serious birth rate problems. Only the much-maligned Chile,[8] which pioneered earnings-linked pensions, has solved the problem by completely withdrawing the state from retirement arrangements. It is absurd to suppose that there is a rationale for state involvement in pensions because of people's high time preferences; they won't save and will become a burden on others. It is the state that has little thought for the future. Most liberal democratic governments have built up huge debts for which future generations will have to pay. The time horizons of most politicians rarely extend beyond the next election.

It is clear that these inefficiencies and injustices occur because the state has extended itself way beyond the original, and laudable, aim of relieving obvious distress. It is now closely involved with most aspects of our lives. Why does it do this? One claim, from moderate socialists, such as C. A. R. Crosland, is that a wide range of state supplied social services increases equality. Leaving aside the unanswerable question of the virtues of equality beyond liberal requirements of impartial, non-discriminatory law, which few would dispute, it is easy to show that state involvement in health, education and pensions is actually productive of greater inequality. Julian Le Grand, himself an egalitarian, has analysed the effect of such policies: they favour the middle classes. As he perceptively observes: 'policies involving subsidies whose distribution is dependent upon people's decision to consume the good or use the service, favour the better off'.[9] Thus heavily subsidised university education is much more likely to be taken up by the middle classes, whose opportunity costs for post-16 education are much lower than those of the poor. The recent expansion of higher education in Britain has made little difference to this behavioural trait. A sincere egalitarian should actually recommend more spending on schooling because that is compulsory. The same reasoning about unequal consumption has been applied to other state services, such as health.

One can only assume that excessive government action in these areas is part of the state's strategy to buy consent. It certainly looks that way in France, where any attempt to reform their ruinous pension scheme causes strikes and disorder. It is often said by historians that early welfare measures, such as the Poor Law, were designed to prevent social disruption (though it is hard to see how the recipients of poor relief could have been a threat to social order). If the purchase of support for government is the rationale for extensive welfare, the people are already beginning to see that so far from being a 'free lunch' excessive welfare is turning out to be a bad deal: it is costly and inefficient, and demands for its privatisation will continue.

Poor relief

Genuine poor relief is one area in which there might be some harmony between minimal statists and the believers in government action but the way it has been handled has provoked classical liberals. It has also proved to be a contentious matter between small-government conservatives and libertarians. It is argued plausibly that poor relief measures, where not financed by any kind of insurance scheme, or work test, have produced moral hazard on the grand scale.[10] The incentive to work is significantly reduced if there is a reward for unemployment. In America, prior to the welfare reforms of 1996,[11] it was thought to contribute to the remarkable rise in unmarried motherhood. It wasn't the generosity of the payments—they were meagre—but the ease with which they could be collected. Conservatives, from the original Poor Law onwards, have been disturbed by cash payments unencumbered by any notion of social duty. Indeed, conservative objections to the welfare state have been as much to do with morality as efficiency.

Thus minimal statists find themselves at odds with conservatives about poverty relief. Even Milton Friedman is not opposed to some but he tries to keep his support for it within the individualist, classical liberal tradition. He believes that there is a charitable instinct in capitalist society; indeed the United States has a remarkable propensity for voluntary donations. Why is there a need for even a minimal welfare state, then? He argues that there are certain inefficiencies in the charity market which make some state action justifiable. In a quotation which has become famous he said: 'I am distressed by the sight of poverty; I am benefited by its alleviation; but I am benefited equally whether I or someone else pays for its alleviation; the benefits of other people's charity partly accrue to me. To put it differently, we might all of us be willing to contribute to the relief of poverty, providing everybody else did.'[12] One person's generosity can make no real difference to the poverty problem. Thus some state relief to the poor makes everybody, including the rich, better off. It is like solving a pollution problem.

Again, his recommendation looks superficially within the minimal state and subjectivist tradition. He suggests a simple cash payment, the Negative Income Tax (NIT), for those whose incomes fall below a certain level. He thinks that the good sense of the electorate will prevent that being bid up so high that it causes serious moral hazard problems. The NIT would require no social duty and its recipients do not even have to spend their money on welfare goods and services, such as unemployment insurance, health insurance or pensions. All this has provoked ire from other minimal statists. Libertarians say that voluntarism is sufficient and that genuine donors do not experience the disincentive to give that Friedman describes: one person's generosity does make a discernible difference. Minimal state conservatives are worried about the effect on personal character that unencumbered poverty relief has.

Minimal statists have a further important objection to extensive poor relief. They maintain that all state welfare has as much to do with the interests of state employees as it has to do with poverty relief. In the language of welfare economics, public employees are 'rent seekers'. In any modern economy economic rent is created. This is income above marginal productivity; that is, what you would get in a fully competitive market economy. Under market conditions, extra income, rent, goes to the successful—be they entrepreneurs or pop stars. Rent is the difference in income they get from their market earnings compared to what they could earn in the next best alternative occupations. Rent, is of course, whittled away by competition. Public employees are normally monopolists and have no serious rival suppliers. Thus they often secure extra earnings compared to what they would get in a competitive market. Public employment is therefore a form of rent seeking, just as is the campaign for import controls.

The organisation of the minimal state

Critics of the extensive state do not confine their strictures, formidable though they are, merely to its policies; they also have well articulated suggestions for improvement. They like to confine the moral input of their suggestions to the advancement of liberty. Although there is, of course, controversy about that concept's meaning, minimal statists tend to adopt the conventional negative view of liberty and suggest institutional methods for its promotion and preservation rather than engage in extensive and intractable moral arguments about freedom.

It is important to stress one feature of the minimal statists' view of liberty which marks them off from more conventional 'social liberals', especially those in America. Classical liberals believe in the symmetry of claims to liberty so that all aspects of freedom are equally important. Economic liberty is on a par with the familiar civil liberties, such as free speech, free movement, the separation of church and state, the right to abortion and so on. In the United States, since the late 1930s, these two aspects of liberty have been separated and economic liberty does not have the same constitutional protection as civil liberty. Also, minimal staters see an intimate connection between liberty and private property, an affiliation that has been almost lost in the modern theory of the state.

Minimal statists have long abandoned the hope of any protection for economic liberty and property from the judiciary or a written constitution—often dismissed as 'parchment protections'. In few countries in the world have they successfully resisted the march of the state. Federal states were thought at one time to provide protection because they have a variety of local jurisdictions and the prospect of competition between them could preserve economic liberty. But most federal systems have experienced an inexorable slide towards power for the central legislature. The Tenth Amendment of the US Constitution offers some formal protection; it states that 'the powers not delegated to the United States by the Constitution, nor prohibited by it to the States, are reserved to the States respectively, or to the people'. Indeed, for much of the nineteenth century the Supreme Court preserved a constitutional balance between the powers of the federal government in Washington and the component states. But the twentieth century saw an inexorable advance of federal power. In 1900 the states spent about 70% of public spending and the federal government about 7%; the rest was by local government. Now the situation is almost exactly reversed. It is true that this was partly brought about by the Sixteenth Amendment (1913), which allowed the federal government to collect an income tax, but much of the decline of the states has been brought about by a complaisant Supreme Court that has not protected economic liberty or states' rights against an expansive central government. Why should the federal government be responsible for Social Security? And how did the Constitutional right of the federal government to regulate commerce between the states (designed originally to prevent inter-state protectionism) become the permission to regulate *intrastate* commerce? The nadir of the compliant Court was reached in a decision in 1985 (*Garcia* v. *San Antonia Metropolitan Transit Authority*) where it was asserted that feder-alism meant merely that the states were represented in Congress. They had no constitutional protection and the Tenth Amendment was senescent.

The European Union is going the same way as the United States, only at a much faster pace. The centralisation began in 1964 with the *Costa* v. *ENEL* decision in which an Italian statute was struck down by the European Court of Justice (ECJ) and the primacy of European law over the law of the member states was asserted. There was no justification for this in the Treaty of Rome. Further advances, such as the ruling that Directives could be directly applied if member states were slow in putting them into domestic law, were made. There was still some doubt as to whether the sovereignty of Parliament in the United Kingdom could ultimately be used against European law even after we signed the Treaty of Rome and formally joined Europe in 1973; the German constitutional court said, in upholding the Treaty of Maastricht in 1994, that Europe was a confederation of autonomous legal systems and that Germany's Basic Law was superior to European law. This is why, to end such uncertainty, the projected European Constitution declares the primacy of European law by treaty.

It might be thought that minimal statists would give a modest welcome to international organisations such as the European Union. After all, aren't they an obstacle to the overweening power of the state, at which minimal statists have directed most of their fire? Does it not mean the end of sovereignty? The European Union does not have many direct tax powers, some of the early decisions of the ECJ were directed against the anti-market tactics of some member states, and is not a commitment to the Four Freedoms, of capital, labour, goods and services, part of the ideology (and treaties) of the Union?

This is not so, because what we are now seeing is not a resurgence of individualism and economic liberty but a new form of statism. Indeed, if the Constitution is ever passed we will have a new state, bigger and more powerful than those it will replace. It will have a legal personality, inter-national status and recognition; and the power to override member states should they get a little too presumptuous. It does not have many direct tax powers yet but the clamour for harmonisation will make them unnecessary. The Union has already expressed displeasure at Ireland's retention of a very low corporation tax, which has been crucial in its attraction of inward capital. What the Union is anxious to prevent is jurisdictional competition in which nations compete with each other in the offer of laws and regulations. Of course, under proper jurisdictional competition the poorer countries will offer less restrictive laws and regulations so as to attract capital from overseas. This is precisely what the richer countries, especially France and Germany, do not want. They can only put off competition for law between states by making certain rules obligatory across all the member states of the European Union. Those poor countries who would object are bought off with regional grants from Brussels. What do we have here if not a state even bigger and more powerful than those that preceded it?

What is relevant to the debate here is the aforementioned theory of rent seeking. It was noticed earlier that competition reduced the rental income of state employees. European Union employees are state employees and will resist any competitive moves that would reduce their emoluments and privileges. The European Commission, whose income derives from super-vising the market, is interested only in preserving economic liberty (emascu-lated though it is) within Europe; it is resolutely opposed to free trade with the outside world, hence the preservation of the ludicrously inefficient Common Agricultural Policy. The only international order consistent with the minimal state is the World Trade Organisation; at least it is dedicated to removing trade barriers world wide. But a minimal statist would say that a country should simply declare free trade, like Hong Kong and, now, Estonia. The resulting competition eventually drives down all protectionism without the need for international organisations, which will succumb to rent seeking eventually, like their national progenitors.

Is there a solution?

The basic problem is simple to state but almost impossible to solve. How do we get those public goods, which are essential for social cooperation, without unintentionally producing an extensive state? And the growth of the state seems ineluctable. This is not just a feature of communism, for majority-rule representative democracy seems to welcome the public realm, despite wide-spread dissatisfaction with public services. Bastiat's 'fictitious entity' does appear to be real, with a life of its own. Minimal statists have made at least two suggestions for producing restraint: one described from experience and some theory, the other purely theoretical. Both have some connection with democracy, albeit somewhat elusive.

The practical suggestion is more *direct* democracy, or extensive use of the referendum on separate issues. That might seem rather odd since that form of government has been historically feared by minimal statists and conserva-tives alike. Will it not lead to rule by the mob, who will use the democratic method to despoil the rich and, if unrestrained, pursue irresponsible redis-tribution? However, a glance at its rival, representative democracy, shows it in a better light. For it is representative democracy that has led to the expansion of the public over the private and produced inefficient and unethical redistribution. The reason for this is not difficult to demonstrate. If we assume that politicians are self-interested utility maximisers who stand for office not to pursue the public good but to earn income they could not earn in the market, to exercise power for its own sake or to display moral vanity, we can easily show the defects of representative democracy. Politicians behave like entrepreneurs,[13] alert to (an electoral) opportunity. Under representative democracy, subject only to majority rule (which rarely has to be fully satisfied to gain office) they will put together a winning coalition of interests by a series of bribes to the electorate, normally by the use of the public purse or some relaxation of the law. In the economic theory of democracy,[14] competing parties aim at the median voter, who, standing midway on a left to right electorate, is likely to be moderate. But most representative democracies have three or more parties and it is relatively easy to win an election. In Britain the winning party rarely achieves more that 44% of the poll. This means that issues are bundled up into a package which will satisfy a collection of interest group demands and not focus on the genuine public interest. Yet, if the issues were to be voted on separately, few of a party's proposals would secure majority support. Only rarely does representative democracy produce long term 'rationality' in the electorate. The modest revulsion against inflation and state economic incompetence in 1970s and 1980s Britain might be one example. The experience certainly pushed Labour to the centre, as the median voter theorem predicts.

We have actual experience of how direct democracy works and it appears to support the minimal statist. I refer to Switzerland, which although it does not always have direct voting on separate issues, does make extensive use of the referendum. And it is the one state which has managed to preserve its federal system. There is considerable power to the component units, the cantons. And, remarkably, the cantons still take a bigger share of public spending than the federal government. The federal government does not even have a prime minister and the executive is composed of all the major parties. In fact, much of the governing is done by the cantons. There is extensive use of the referendum at cantonal and federal levels. Any new law by the federal government is put to a referendum. This is perhaps the major reason why government is still relatively small in Switzerland. But not all is perfect even there. The cantons voluntarily surrendered their welfare powers to the federal government some decades ago. Of course, welfare spending then increased substantially beyond what the average Swiss citizen wanted. The cantons are trying now to recapture their power over welfare.

The purely theoretical model of the limited state is not unrelated to the Swiss experience: it endeavours to make choice in institutions work in the same way as it does in the product market.[15] It holds that people should be given the opportunity simply to leave polities that have extended public goods beyond what is desired. The resulting shifts in population to low cost areas would encourage a generalised reduction in public activities. It would probably work better in a genuinely federal union where exit costs are not prohibitively high and where cultural and linguistic differences are not great enough to make exit too cumbersome. It works to some extent in the United States, where the English language and the adoption of the common law (outside Louisiana) have made the component states to some extent culturally similar. Of course, it is impossible to escape from the depredations of individual liberty and the market which have already taken place at the federal level. But it is a theoretically plausible model which indicates how the extensive state might be avoided. It posits the state as a kind of 'club'[16] which we are free to join (or leave) according to the services it provides. The services offered by such clubs could extend across familiar political boundaries so that people would not actually have to leave. It could be called the Tesco theory of the state.

There is, though, a problem in all versions of competitive jurisdictions. They have to be nested in a given set of general rules which will *not* be open to competition. These will normally relate to civil liberty. No minimal statist or libertarian would countenance a club that offered slavery or, more likely, discriminated against a particular group. It is not satisfactory to say that the market would never produce such phenomena or that the victims could always leave and join a different club. Something unpleasant might emerge and it would be unfair to impose heavy costs on those compelled to leave.

There is a further economic problem with most versions of club government or fully competitive jurisdictions. What if the component states of a federal union decided to use their liberty to impose protectionism themselves? Indeed, in the early days of the European Economic Community, the ECJ enforced the Four Freedoms effectively against recalcitrant states which used their then autonomy to impose protectionism. It might take the market alone a very long time to correct such errors. Even if basic freedoms were nominally acknowledged by the component units of such a federal union they might restrict imports by subtle methods. They need not introduce tariffs but could produce the same effect by various forms of 'quality control'. It might take an experienced court to adjudicate on whether an action was in breach of the basic rules. Courts are not likely to be reliable in this area.

Whatever the difficulties it is certainly the case that if a serious move towards the minimal state were to be made it would have to be along these lines. Experience suggests that competition, rather than written documents interpreted by unpredictable courts, is the best protection of liberty and the minimal state. Direct democracy can be interpreted as a species of the competitive genus: at least choice on individual issues gives the voter more choice than does voting on a bundle of different policies.

Notes

1 See Norman Barry, 'Estonia moves to liberty', *Ideas on Liberty*, vol. 53, no. 5, May 2004.
2 *The Nature and Causes of the Wealth of Nations*, edited by R. H. Campbell and A. S. Skinner, Oxford, Clarendon Press, 1976, p. 456. First published 1776.
3 In 'The state', in George B. Huszar, ed., *Selected Essays on Political Economy*,

Irvington-on-Hudson, Foundation for Economic Education, 1995. First published 1848.

4 H. L. A. Hart, *The Concept of Law*, Oxford, Clarendon Press, 1961, pp. 193–200.

5 See Norman Barry, *An Introduction to Modern Political Theory*, fourth edition, London, Macmillan, 2000, chapter 3.

6 See Anthony de Jasay, *The State*, Oxford, Basil Blackwell, 1985, pp. 232–43.

7 Norman Barry, 'The state, pensions and the philosophy of welfare', *Journal of Social Policy*, vol. 14, 1985, pp. 468–90.

8 See Norman Barry, 'Pensions: A worldwide but avoidable crisis', *Ideas on Liberty*, vol. 53, October 2003, pp. 22–6.

9 Julian Le Grand, *The Strategy of Equality*, London, Allen and Unwin, 1982, p. 46.

10 See Charles Murray, *Losing Ground: America's Social Policy 1950–80*, New York, Basic Books, 1984.

11 Personal Responsibility and Work Opportunity Reconciliation Act, 1996.

12 Milton Friedman, *Capitalism and Freedom*, Chicago, University of Chicago Press, 1962, p. 190.

13 Joseph Schumpeter, *Capitalism, Socialism and Democracy*, London, Allen and Unwin, 1954.

14 A. Downs, *An Economic Theory of Democracy*, New York, Harper and Row, 1957.

15 Charles Tiebout, 'A pure theory of local expenditure', *Journal of Political Economy*, vol. 64, 1956, pp. 416–24.

16 See J. Buchanan, 'An economic theory of clubs', *Economica*, vol. 32, 1965, pp. 1–14.

Neo-liberalism and the Theory of the State: From *Wohlfahrtsstaat* to *Rechtsstaat*

RAYMOND PLANT

MY AIM in this chapter is to set out as clearly as possible the conception of the nature, scope and role of the state held by neo- or economic liberals. My characterisation of this theory of the state is a composite one and has been built up from materials to be found in many neo-liberal writers and political thinkers such as F. A. von Hayek, M. Friedman, J. Buchanan, G. Tullock, W. Niskanen, J. Gray (in an earlier phase of his thought), S. Brittan and A. de Jasay;[1] politicians such as Lord Joseph, N. Lawson, N. Ridley and E. Powell (in some respects);[2] and from pamphlets and reports issued by think tanks such as the Institute for Economic Affairs, the Mont Pelerin Society and the Adam Smith Institute. So it may be that no one individual represented in the materials assembled here would agree with every detail of what is being called the neo-liberal conception of the state; nevertheless the conception that I shall outline is, I believe, in broad terms correct. Indeed, I regard this conception of the state as being both coherent and powerful and one that has still not elicited a full response either from social democrats or for that matter from *social* liberals.[3]

In my understanding of the term, 'neo-liberal' is used to designate those who have sought to update and rethink some of the tenets of 'classical' liberalism associated historically with figures such as A. Smith, R. Cobden and J. Bright. My subtitle is significant in that it reflects what I believe to be the very important influence of Hayek in the development of this account of the state and the fact that it has been deeply shaped by a response to the characteristic features of the post Second World War welfare state. The critique of the central features of that sort of state, supported as it was by social democrats and social liberals, lies at the heart of the neo-liberals' development of their own distinctive conception.

There is a view that whether we like it or not globalisation with all its related features is going to lead to a world in which the neo-liberal conception of limited government, combined with free markets and a residual (if any) role for the welfare state, is going to be the dominant state form. Indeed, not long ago in the *New Left Review* Perry Anderson called neo-liberalism the most successful ideology in modern history. Its success has been seen at least in large part to do with changes in the global economy which have led to what Phillip Bobbitt called 'the market state' in his influential *The Shield of Achilles*,[4] although he sees a wider range of factors than globalisation at work in the

 Published by Blackwell Publishing Ltd, 9600 Garsington Road, Oxford OX4 2DQ, UK and 350 Main Street, Malden, MA 02148, USA

success of this state paradigm. In this chapter I will not try to assess these sorts of arguments about modern international political economy which might be thought to favour the emergence (or perhaps re-emergence) of the neo-liberal state. I will concentrate upon what might be called the political philosophy of the neo-liberal state and, as I have suggested, it is sensible to start with the critique of the welfare state because the neo-liberals' own view of the state has grown up in the last generation out of the critique of the welfare state.

Freedom

It is perhaps best to begin with two of what might be thought of as the most abstract issues in play between the neo-liberals and the social democrats and social liberals, namely the nature of freedom and the nature of social justice. It is no accident that two of the foundational texts of neo-liberal thought reflect the importance of these two fundamental values. I refer to *The Constitution of Liberty* by Friedrich von Hayek, published in 1960, and *The Mirage of Social Justice*, the second volume of *Law, Legislation and Liberty*, by the same author and published in 1976. I shall begin the analysis with the idea of freedom because it is certainly arguable that 'new' or 'social' liberalism grew up in the UK in the 1880s partly as the result of a view that the link between 'classical' or as it was called 'old' liberalism, with its emphasis on limited government and free markets and a wholly negative view of liberty, was a mistake.[5] In the view of new liberals such as T. H. Green, A. Toynbee, Sir Henry Jones, L. A. Hobhouse and, via these thinkers, politicians like H. H. Asquith and R. B. Haldane, freedom had to be understood in a 'more subtle sense', to quote Lord Haldane.[6] This more subtle sense was to understand freedom not only in terms of the absence of coercion, that is to say negative liberty, but also in terms of ability or capacity to do things and to make the best of oneself. If freedom is understood in terms of ability, then as the new liberals argued and as Hayek recognises in Chapter 1 of *The Constitution of Liberty*, an argument in favour of the state taking responsibility for at least some level of the welfare of citizens could be mounted in terms of the defence of liberty, which after all is the central liberal value.

If ability implies opportunity and access to resources with which to achieve the ends that one has as a moral being then, on this view, a liberal state as the defender of liberty has to be concerned with the distribution of resources that will reasonably satisfy the claims of ability and opportunity. Hence a concern with positive liberty will naturally also imply a concern with distributive justice: that is to say, with access to that bundle of resources and opportunities which individuals should have in order to realise positive freedom. Given that the market cannot seemingly secure such resources to individuals on a predictable basis, never mind as social rights as they eventually came to be perceived, then it came to be argued that the state has to ensure that individuals have a just share of the resources necessary to secure their positive freedom. In this way, freedom and social justice go together. It has been central to the neo-liberal critique of the social liberal and social democratic state that this positive view of freedom is fundamentally mistaken and that social or distributive justice is either an undesirable or, more radically, a *meaningless* ideal. If these two claims can be sustained then they would amount to a central blow against two of the foundational values of the welfare state. So we need now to turn to that critique.

The critique of the idea of positive liberty is clear and straightforward. First of all it is argued that freedom and ability cannot be the same thing, since no one is able to do all that he or she is free to do. I am free to do everything that I am not currently prevented by others from doing. This will turn out to be an indefinitely large number of things. However, it does not matter how rich and powerful or how intelligent or resourceful I am, it still remains the case that I am able to do only a small number of things that I am free to do. Hence freedom and ability cannot be the same thing. A liberal state in defending liberty should be concerned to prevent the coercion of one person by another, and this can be done by the rule of law enforcing a rule of mutual non-coercion—that is to say, negative liberty. It should not be done by a welfare state securing to individuals resources to enable them to do what they are free to do. There is no way in which abilities, capacities and powers can be equalised, and therefore if freedom is understood at least in part in terms of ability then we can never attain the liberal ideal of equal freedom, an ideal which can be attained if by freedom we mean mutual non-coercion.

The same point applies to opportunity. On the neo-liberal view, equality of opportunity has to be understood negatively; that is to say, the removal of those obstacles placed in the way of individuals by the intentional actions of others. It does not mean equality of opportunity in a positive sense, of securing to individuals resources to make them able to take those opportunities afforded in the negative sense of non-discrimination. It is central to the neo-liberal case that equality of opportunity in the negative sense can be achieved by laws against non-discrimination and other forms of coercion, and this role for the law is compatible with the idea of the rule of law in the sense of impartiality and treating like cases in like manner. A positive idea of opportunity seeking to equalise the ability to take advantage of opportunities cannot be secured to individuals by rules which are compatible with the idea of the rule of law—a point which I will develop further later. It can be seen already, however, that in the neo-liberal view a welfare state (*wohlfahrtsstaat*) cannot be a state bound by the rule of law (*rechtsstaat*).

In both the cases of liberty and of opportunity I have referred to coercion and to obstacles put in one's way by the intentional actions of others. Obviously, any conception of freedom—whether positive or negative—is going to have to invoke some idea of coercion. Indeed, the idea of coercion is central to any account of the nature and scope of the state. Neo-liberals have clear ideas about this which again strike at the heart of the social liberal and social democratic view of the relation between freedom and markets. For the neo-liberal, coercion has to be understood as an intentional act, such as an act of prevention or discrimination. Hence A coerces B when he or she gets B to do something that B would otherwise not have done or gets B to refrain from doing something that otherwise he or she would have done. Freedom as negative freedom is the absence of this kind of coercion and can be attained in ways compatible with the idea of the rule of law via a rule of mutual non-coercion.

However, this point cuts deeper. As we have seen, positive freedom implies the idea that the state rather than the market should have the final responsibility for securing resources to individuals in a fair way—a task that the market cannot perform. Without this role for the state, individuals left to the vagaries of the market would find that their lack of resources infringed their (positive) freedom. So on this view, markets left to their own devices infringe liberty because they cannot guarantee to individuals that bundle of goods necessary for positive freedom. The neo-liberal view of liberty precludes this. First of all for the obvious reason that neo-liberals reject the idea of positive liberty, but also because of the fact that since in their view freedom can only be infringed by intentional actions, market outcomes cannot infringe the freedom of any particular individual because these outcomes are not in fact intended or foreseen by anyone. In a market, millions of people intentionally buy and sell for all the particular reasons that they have, and at any point this market produces results for individuals: some will be rich and some will be poor. This is, however, an unintended consequence of market behaviour and indeed, given the complexity of the transactions, cannot be foreseen. No doubt in particular instances individuals may be cheated and defrauded, but this is an interference with negative liberty which can be attended to by laws enforcing mutual non-coercion. The overall aggregate outcomes of markets are unintended and therefore the resources which people do or do not have cannot be regarded either as a restriction or an improvement in their liberty. So, given that coercion has to be intentional, market outcomes are not coercive and do not limit liberty. Or in Keith Joseph's clear words in his book *Equality*, 'Poverty is not unfreedom.'

So it is the duty of the state to protect negative liberty, and its role in respect of liberty and markets is to ensure the framework of mutual non-coercion. This will in turn entail laws about contract keeping, promise keeping, laws against discrimination and laws against fraud, theft, negligence (when there is a clear victim). It also entails that it is impossible to produce a distributive welfare state compatible with the rule of law, at least in terms of the protection of liberty.

Justice and social justice

These issues naturally lead us to arguments about social or distributive justice. It might be argued, as for example J. Rawls does in *A Theory of Justice*,[7] that the protection and securing of justice is a central role for the state since justice is, as he says, 'the first virtue of institutions'. Does this concern apply also to social or distributive justice? As I have said, one strand of thought in favour of distributive justice has been the argument about liberty: that each individual should have a fair share of basic or generic resources without which their positive liberty is infringed. So there is a clear link between the issue of freedom and the distributive state. The neo-liberals, however, offer a sustained critique of the distributive social democratic/liberal state.

The first of these arguments is implicit in what has gone before. Neo-liberals argue that injustice can only result from an *intentional* act. This marks the difference between injustice and bad luck or misfortune. We do not regard a genetic handicap as an injustice; we do not regard the effects of the weather, in themselves, as an injustice. The reason according to neo-liberals is easy to discern. Genetic disorders and the weather are not the result of intentional processes (discounting a malevolent deity). That is why they are matters of misfortune, not injustice. The state indeed has a responsibility to maintain justice and to correct injustice but this responsibility does not extend to rectifying the outcomes of markets, because these outcomes for reasons already given are to be regarded as unintended. We can bear no collective moral responsibility for the unintended outcomes of markets any more than we do for the genetic lottery or the weather. Poverty as the result of free market operation is, like the genetic lottery and the weather, a misfortune not an injustice. There is not and cannot be an obligation on government to rectify misfortune otherwise the obligations on the state would be irrationally wide, since misfortunes and bad luck are so endemic and pervasive in human life and there would be no consensus about which should be rectified. So the outcomes of markets do not imply strict obligations on governments in terms of justice to intervene to correct the outcomes of markets. Benevolence, charity and altruism are the appropriate personal responses to misfortune, not state action in pursuit of distributive justice. Individuals do not have a right to be taken off the wheel of fortune, as Keith Joseph put this point.

So if we look at the moral basis of the distributive state we can see in the neo-liberal view that the alleged moral case for the welfare state in terms of justice is not compelling. There are other arguments at work in this critique of social justice too. One of the most important which looms large particularly in the work of Hayek is the idea that values, including those attached to the idea of social justice, are subjective. In a sense, at best social justice is what Rawls called a *concept*: a thin and uninterpreted idea. This concept leads to the development of a range of possible *conceptions*. That is to say, we could utilise many radically different criteria of social justice which would yield mutually incompatible forms of distribution. Goods, services, benefits and burdens could be distributed according to desert, equality, need, contribution, entitlement, ownership of the means of production, the marginal product of labour and no doubt others too. All of these can be understood as possible versions of social justice, and given the subjectivity of values we have no rational way of arbitrating between them. Even if, *per impossibile*, we were able to fix upon a particular conception such as distribution according to desert, this does not help very much since the idea of desert is internally complex and probably interminably disputable. It is perhaps in this sense most of all that social justice is a mirage, even if we accepted—which in the view of the neo-liberals we should not for the reasons given above—that social justice is a valid moral ideal.

Interest groups

The pursuit of social justice leads to two further baneful effects on the role of the state understood as a distributive device. The first is that if the state is seen as a mechanism of distribution in a context in which there is no distributive consensus because moral values are seen as subjective, then it is inevitable that interest groups will be brought into being who will pursue rent-seeking behaviour to gain rights, privileges and resources from the state. Such interest groups will inevitably form coalitions in order to extract what from their own subjective points of view is seen as their 'due' from government. In these circumstances the state is very likely to fall victim to a current coalition of the most powerful interest groups in society. So, on this view, far from social justice being some kind of noble ideal it rather becomes a fig leaf to disguise rent-seeking behaviour, with the result that the poor whom social justice and the distributive state are supposed to help will be the most likely group to suffer as a result. This approach offers a major challenge to any easy assumptions about the benign aspects of the pluralist theories of democracy popular in the postwar period and corporatist approaches to economic management. This argument is set out in a very compelling way by S. Brittan in *A Restatement of Economic Liberalism* and in *The Role and Limits of Government: Essays in Political Economy*.

Bureaucracy and the neo-liberal state

The second effect is that a distributive state is bound to be very bureaucratic, charging bureaucracies of various kinds to distribute resources and services according to whatever is the currently preferred criterion of social justice. However, given the earlier points made about the subjectivity of value, it is argued that the distributive state cannot be made properly subject to the rule of law since it is not possible to write rules of law which will secure to individuals what are supposed to be their just deserts or to meet their needs, or whatever the distributive principle is held to be. This means that those who work in welfare bureaucracies will have a very great deal of discretionary power. This power is, in principle, going to be unaccountable because there cannot be substantive as opposed to procedural rules of law that can constrain that power in the particular circumstances, which will be highly contextualised and individualised, in which this discretionary power is in fact used.

Hence the distributive welfare state places at the centre of its operation power that is in principle unaccountable.

This point then connects with another very important driver in the neo-liberal theory of the state, namely their economic theory of bureaucratic behaviour, which derives from the Public Choice school of economics, located particularly at the Universities of Chicago (Tullock) and Virginia (Buchanan). This school applies general neo-classical economic theory to the behaviour of bureaucracies. The central idea is that of the rational economic man (or woman) who will seek to maximise his or her utilities in whatever circumstances they find themselves. Utility maximising behaviour is not confined to markets but can in fact be found in any area of human endeavour including bureaucracies. So bureaucracies and bureaucrats (remember that most neo-liberals are methodological individualists) will seek to maximise their utilities. Such behaviour in markets serves the interests of customers and shareholders of firms, since utility maximisation for the individual working within the firm can only be secured if that behaviour serves the interests and desires of customers and shareholders. If ultimately it does not serve the interests of the customers then the firm is likely to go bankrupt. Thus the pursuit of private self-interest in a market context serves the needs of the customer of the firm.

In the public sector, according to the neo-liberal, the motivation is the same, namely to maximise utility, but this is against a background in which there is not the constraint and the discipline of the threat of bankruptcy. Hence utility maximising behaviour is likely to involve increasing the size, scope and sphere of responsibility of the bureau and through that the salaries and the status of those who work within it. This behaviour is relatively unconstrained compared with the private market sector, since there is not the possibility of bankruptcy; the behaviour cannot be made accountable via detailed rules of law because these cannot cover the highly individualised cases with which welfare bureaucracies have to deal. Also, the elasticity of criteria of just distribution, particularly the elasticity of the idea of need, which plays a central role in underpinning the mission of the public sector, fuels the growth of bureaucracy both by the 'discovery' of new needs for which the state should assume responsibility and new and frequently more costly ways of satisfying old needs. Hence, unlike the social liberal and the social democrat, the neo-liberal is very unlikely to repose much faith in the ideal of the 'public service' ethic or ethos as a means of constraining the behaviour of public service bureaucracies. Individuals in the public sector do not step into a different ethical realm like Platonic Guardians or Hegel's members of the 'universal class' whose own self-interest coincides with the public interest. On the contrary, public officials maximise utility like those in markets but without the constraints and disciplines of the market. This leads neo-liberals to argue that as much as possible of the existing public sector should be taken to the market and made subject to market disciplines. This approach to the economics of bureaucracy has been taken furthest by Niskanen, particularly in *Bureaucracy and Representative Government*. The ideas in this book gained political attention in the UK via his Hobart paper 'Bureaucracy: servant or master?' for the Institute of Economic Affairs published in 1973, which had a laudatory introduction by Nicholas Ridley, one of the leading neo-liberal politicians within the Conservative Party. Its ideas are also reflected in Nigel Lawson's 1980 lecture *The New Conservatism*.

Rights

It might be thought that a central role for the state is to be found in the protection of rights. So what is the neo-liberal approach to this issue? In fact it is a further issue of contention between the social liberal/democrat and the neo-liberal and flows in a sense as a consequence of the previous points taken together—that is to say, a vigorous critique of social and economic rights. In the view of the neo-liberal, rights should be seen as civil and political rights and construed as far as possible in negative terms. This is partly because of the philosophical point that rights are supposed to protect a sphere of individual freedom and that freedom is to be understood according to the neo-liberal as freedom from coercion. Rights are supposed to define a range of illegitimate interferences of one person with another. One way of putting the point is that they elaborate the idea of freedom as mutual non-coercion. So the right to life is a right not to be killed, not a right to the means to life; a right to property is understood as a right not to have property interfered with, not a right to own property; the right to work is understood as a right not to be prevented from working—for example by discrimination or illegal picketing—and is not a right to a job, and so on. Social and economic rights, on the other hand, are defective centrally because they protect a mistaken and over-extended view of liberty, namely positive liberty or freedom as ability which, as we have seen, neo-liberals reject.

There is, however, another central argument to the neo-liberal approach to the critique of social and economic rights. This is the idea that such rights cannot be genuine rights because they are inherently rights to scarce resources: the services of a doctor, a hospital, a teacher, a school, etc. These cannot be categorical rights because there will always be limits on the supply of such goods, given the elastic nature of the demand for them which lies behind the idea of such rights. Negative rights, on the other hand, can always be treated as categorical rights because the duties which they imply unlike those implied by social and economic rights can always in fact be fulfilled. The reason is that negative rights yield duties of forbearance; not to coerce, not to kill, assault, defraud, interfere, etc. As such, they are duties to abstain from doing these forbidden things and as forbearances, as forms of inaction, they are costless and can always be performed. This it is claimed is in stark contrast to positive social and economic rights, which are intrinsically rights to resources that are always in scarce supply. Nor will it save social and economic rights in the view of the neo-liberal to claim that such rights are not categorical but rather rights to a fair share of social goods like the services of doctors and hospitals, because that brings the issue of social or distributive justice back into the picture as determining what is a fair share to satisfy the claim of right. As we have seen, the neo-liberal rejects the idea of social justice and, given that rejection, ideas of fairness cannot be imported into rights to rescue social and economic rights from their impossible to realise, seemingly categorical nature.

There is an additional and politically important argument against social and economic rights deployed by neo-liberals, namely that against the assumptions of those who believe in welfare rights, far from creating strong and independent individuals who stand up for their rights and use the resources procured by those rights (that is, 'entitlements') this rights-based culture has caused a great deal of dependency on the state. These 'rights' cut off the link between income and work and give people an incentive not to engage in the labour market and to live indefinitely on benefits, if they are prepared to accept a lowish standard of living. This in turn has bad effects, creating a sense of isolation, a detachment from sources of knowledge and improvement that comes from being in the world of work, and a weakening of ideas about social obligation.

This kind of diagnosis can lead in two directions. The first is in more of a neo-conservative way than a neo-liberal one and is perhaps best exemplified by Lawrence Mead's work *Beyond Entitlement*,[8] published in 1986. The central thesis of this argument is that benefits should be tied either to working or to engaging in workfare or learnfare schemes. This requires the state to be prepared to hold and to enforce social obligations and in some way or another at a national or a local level to become a provider of at least resources if not services for workfare and learnfare schemes. It is not clear that this approach is at all compatible with neo-liberal principles about the role, scope and nature of the state. The alternative is that proposed by Charles Murray, who argues against welfare rights in his *In Pursuit of Happiness and Good Government*[9] on the grounds that 'free lunches don't nourish' and is in favour not of the Mead approach but rather of removing state support altogether so that those out of work for whatever reason will be forced by circumstance to seek help from relatives, neighbours, friends, churches and charities. The degree of social pressure at the local face-to-face level that will be able to be exerted on the workless in these circumstances will give the workless and the work shy strong incentives to go back to work. This would seem to follow more clearly from this diagnosis of what is wrong with welfare rights when conjoined with arguments about the nature of justice and charity discussed earlier.

So there is a complete tie up between neo-liberal views about liberty, the rejection of social justice and the rejection of social and economic rights. The protection of negative liberty via a strict rule of law is possible because liberty is negative liberty and rights are negative rights; both imply duties of non-coercion which are always capable of being fulfilled and therefore can be subjected to a clear rule of law. This is not so with positive liberty, positive rights and social justice. The links between negative liberty and positive rights and the rejection of positive freedom, social and economic rights and the idea of social justice are central to the neo-liberal ideal of the state as a *rechtsstaat*.

It has to be said in passing that Hayek does think that there is a case to be made for at least a minimal or residual welfare safety net—an argument that he develops in *The Constitution of Liberty*. However, two things remain obscure in his account. First of all he wants to argue that there is a categorical difference between a welfare state understood as a safety net and a welfare state understood as an instrument of social justice, a point also made by Keith Joseph in *Stranded on the Middle Ground*. This might be doubted. The first reason is that a safety net has to be fixed at some level, and if this is not going to be wholly arbitrary it is likely to be related to some idea of basic needs. This in itself is problematic for Hayek: why should there be a social consensus about basic needs and what they require for their satisfaction when it is central to his argument against social justice that there is no consensus about social values? The second point is that the idea of needs is rather elastic. Such a welfare state even at the level at which Hayek envisages it is going to have to be delivered by a bureaucracy which will find a good deal of discretion in relation to elastic needs. If this is so, how far is Hayek's own account of the welfare state compatible with his own account of the rule of law? In addition, given the point that welfare bureaucrats are able to exploit the vagueness of welfare concepts like needs to increase their range and scope, what will prevent welfare bureaucrats in a Hayekian welfare state from bidding up the idea of need? If this is done there will be very little difference between a Hayekian welfare state and one based upon ideas about social justice.

The market state and the market order

All of this naturally spills over into the political economy of neo-liberalism, and here I shall give a sketch of this in so far as it bears upon the role and the competence of the state. Perhaps the first point to make, drawing upon the philosophical issues that have gone before, is to say that the neo-liberal state is a *nomocratic* state rather than a *telocratic* one. That is to say, it is concerned with the structure of the framework of non-coercion and rights that have to be in place within which invidividuals can pursue their own good in their own way so long as in pursuing that good they do not interfere with the freedom of others to do the same. A telocratic state, however, is concerned not only with structures and procedures but rather with ends such as social justice, and will search for institutions and policies that will secure such collective ends. It is concerned with virtues, not just rules.

For the neo-liberal, collective ends should be seen in terms of the structure, not in terms of collective goals of society as a whole. The first thing that this entails for the neo-liberal is a rejection of the idea of planning to achieve the aims of a telocratic state. This planning could be seen either in terms of the centralised planning of the postwar socialist states or of France, or indeed in a much more limited way of using Keynesian demand management techniques to seek to engineer supposedly desirable social outcomes. There are no collective outcomes to be desired and therefore these should not be the object of state policy. I shall not go into the detailed critique of centralised planning developed by von Mises and Hayek because in a sense these issues are subordinate to the philosophical point whose roots I have tried to uncover, that there should not be collective aims but only a set of rules of law to define in detail what mutual non-coercion actually entails in practice. Suffice it to say for the moment that the critique of planning makes the role of the entrepreneur central to the political economy of neo-liberalism. If planning is both undesirable as well as epistemically impossible, as Mises and Hayek believed, then the market should be allowed the greatest possible degree of freedom, partly because as we have seen there is no collective moral reason to interfere with it and because the market can transmit information about prices and costs which governments and bureaucracies are endemically incapable of doing because of the dispersed and fragmented nature of knowledge in modern society. Given this fragmentation of knowledge, then entrepreneurship plays an absolutely essential role in utilising the price information transmitted by the market and the fragmented knowledge available to individuals that is not available to government. Therefore it is essential to economic prosperity in the view of the neo-liberal that the state should not do anything by way of taxation or regulation which is going to stifle the capacity for entrepreneurship and interfere with the way in which the market works as the most efficient conduit of information both between individuals and firms.

Of course, committed as they are to collective ends, particularly in terms of the idea of social justice, social liberals /social democrats are committed both to a substantial public sector as the vehicle for the delivery of those goods understood to be essential for social justice and to the level of taxation needed to fund this. Here, perhaps, we reach the heart of fundamentally different views as between the orthodox Keynesian postwar social democrat and late twentieth century neo-liberals. If we take C. A. R. Crosland as the paradigmatic postwar social democrat we can see the difference of approach in a graphic way. In his *The Future of Socialism*, published in 1956, Crosland produced the definitive text of postwar social democracy, and in the early 1970s just at the beginning of the revival of neo-liberal ideas he restated a central element of his case in the Fabian pamphlet *Social Democracy in Europe*.[10] Here he argues the following claims: that the central aim of social democracy is social justice understood in an egalitarian, indeed in a Rawlsian way; that central to the achievement of an improvement in the relative position of the worst-off members of society is economic growth; that economic growth will allow for fiscal dividends which can be invested in the public sector, which will improve the relative position of the worst off while maintaining the absolute position of the better off. It is in Crosland's view essential to maintain this absolute position of the better off if one is to mobilise a majority behind social democratic policies.

Most of this from a neo-liberal perspective is precisely wrong. First of all, the size of the public sector needed to deliver the illusory ideal of social justice will militate against the economic growth on which Crosland relies. The tax levels needed to sustain the public sector will have a negative effect on work incentives. The financing of the public sector by borrowing is likely to crowd out investment in the productive private sector. Both of these will have a negative impact on growth, which is the engine of egalitarianism for Crosland. Secondly, it is false to claim that investment in the public sector is on the whole differentially in the interest of the poorest sections of society and that generally the middle classes have been the greatest gainers from the welfare state. So even as a policy in pursuit of a misguided aim this approach embodies a bad choice of policies. Finally, we should abandon the idea of relative poverty and, in a sense, put Crosland's distributive point almost exactly the opposite way round. That is to say, what we should be concerned about is not so much the relative position of the worst off (that is, the gap between the worst off and other groups in society) but rather their absolute position. The aim of policy should be to make the worst off better off next year in their own terms than they were this year. This can take place and indeed in the neo-liberal view is most likely to take place if we remain resolutely unconcerned about their relative position. The reason for this is that growing inequality, which is what a growing relative gap means, will still be to the advantage of the worst off because the trickle-down or echelon advance effect of the market will in fact make the worst off better off in real terms, even though the better off have increased their differential position. Hence we should be concerned about the real or absolute position of the worst off and the relative position of the better off, and by improving the relative position of the latter we shall release the dynamism of the market and improve the former—precisely the opposite of Croslandite social democracy.[11]

It might be thought that this latter set of arguments have moved us some way away from the more central arguments about the nature of the state, but this would be a mistake. For the neo-liberal, I believe, these claims about economic performance are central to the idea of the legitimacy of the neo-liberal state. The reason for this is fairly obvious. If the neo-liberal is not holding out any hope or desirability for the normative legitimacy of the state to arise through ideas like the collective pursuit of values such as social justice, and if the neo-liberal believes that goal-directed collective action is illegitimate, then what is it that can secure the legitimacy of the economic liberal state? Given that this state is essentially a set of procedural rules to facilitate mutual non-coercion and the maintenance of the free market as the best means to economic prosperity, then it is vital that the claims made for the conjunction of the neo-liberal state and the free market actually produce material prosperity, particularly for the worst-off groups for whom the question of the legitimacy of the neo-liberal state is the most pressing. This point is well understood by Hayek, who on page 74 of *The Mirage of Social Justice* makes the point that there is a real problem for the legitimacy of the market order (which is conjoined to the neo-liberal state), in that the most compelling justification for the market that people in general seem to entertain is that it rewards the deserving. In Hayek's view this is false, because this would make the market an instrument of a collective value or social justice—namely in this case that 'desert should be rewarded'. Rather, the market does not reward according to any principle at all, or to put the point in Fred Hirsch's words it is 'in principle unprincipled'. If this central facet of the neo-liberal order has to secure legitimacy precisely because it does not produce results according to any principle, then clearly there is a problem which Hayek is candid enough to state:

It is therefore a real dilemma to what extent we ought to encourage in the young the belief that when they really try they will succeed, or should rather emphasise that inevitably some unworthy will succeed and some worthy fail—whether we ought to allow the views of those groups to prevail with whom the over-confidence in the appropriate reward of the able and industrious is strong and who in consequence will do much that benefits the rest, and whether without such partly erroneous beliefs the large numbers will tolerate actual differences in rewards which will be based only partly on achievement and partly on mere chance.

So it might be thought that if this is right the neo-liberal state depends on a kind of noble lie: that it is assumed to do one thing, namely reward desert, when in fact it does something else, namely not to reward according to any principle at all. Of course, the sensible move for the neo-liberal who was impressed by Hayek's candour here would be to shift the burden of legitimacy to the political structure itself, the framework of mutual non-coercion. However, that would mean detaching the justification of this structure from the economic benefits it is thought (falsely, in Hayek's view) to bring to particular groups of people. This is not in principle impossible to do but it does mean that the justification of the limited state of neo-liberalism has to depend on not seeing it as purely instrumental to economic perform-ance and as having some positive value of its own. Naturally enough, in these circumstances the concentration will be on the neo-liberal state as a frame-work for freedom. The problem here is that some neo-liberals including Hayek, I believe, see freedom itself as instrumental to market performance, as he strongly suggests in Chapter 2 of *The Constitution of Liberty*: 'If we are not free then the market will not be dynamic, fragmented knowledge will not get used, and entrepreneurs will not flourish.' This brings back again the justification of the market order if it is 'in principle unprincipled', and it might be thought to be quite dangerous for the normative legitimacy of the neo-liberal state to depend on a market with the character attributed to it by at least some neo-liberal thinkers. I say some because it would not apply for example to Robert Nozick in so far as he can be regarded as a neo-liberal, since for Nozick individual freedom and autonomy is a basic good and the rights that flow from this are inviolable as he argues in *Anarchy, State and*

Utopia.[12] These rights are best embodied in a market order, but it would appear for Nozick that even if the market order did not in fact maximise material benefits or efficiency it would still have moral and political legitimacy as the embodiment of inviolable rights. However, this argument is not open to Hayek. Hence I do not think that it is possible to understand the nature and legitimacy of the neo-liberal state without linking it to the distinctive neo-liberal understanding of the market order. So far this has in many ways been its strength but, as Hayek sees, in certain circumstances it could be a fatal weakness if people demand more from the state than the procedural state of neo-liberalism can give them.

Notes

1 See F. A. von Hayek, *The Constitution of Liberty*, London, Routledge, 1960, and *The Mirage of Social Justice*, London, Routledge, 1976; M. Friedman, *Capitalism and Freedom*, Chicago, Chicago University Press, 1962; J. Buchanan,'Why does government grow?', in T. E. Borcheding, ed., *Budgets and Bureaucrats: The Sources of Government Growth*, Durham NC, Duke University Press,1977; G. Tullock, *The Politics of Bureaucracy*, Washington DC, Public Affairs Press, 1965; W. Niskanen, *Bureaucracy and Representative Government*, Chicago, Aldine-Atherton, 1971; J. Gray, *Hayek on Liberty*, Oxford, Basil Blackwell, 1984, and 'Classical liberalism, positional goods and the politicisation of poverty', in A. Ellis and K. Kumar, eds, *Dilemmas of Liberal Democracy*, London, Tavistock, 1983; S. Brittan, *A Restatement of Economic Liberalism Basingstoke*, Macmillan, 1973, and *The Role and Limits of Government: Essays in Political Economy*, Hounslow, Maurice Temple Smith, 1984; A. de Jasay, *The State*, Oxford, Blackwell, 1985, and *Choice, Contract and Consent*, London, Institute of Economic Affairs, 1991.
2 K. Joseph and J. Sumption, *Equality*, London, John Murray, 1979; K. Joseph, *Stranded on the Middle Ground*, London, Centre for Policy Studies, 1976; N. Lawson, *The New Conservatism*, London, Centre for Policy Studies, 1980; N. Ridley, 'Foreword' to W. Niskanen, *Bureaucracy: Servant or Master?*, London, Institute of Economic Affairs, 1973; E. Powell, *Still to Decide*, London, Elliot Right Way Books,1972.
3 For my own attempt to do this see K. Hoover and R. Plant, *Conservative Capitalism in Britain and the United States*, London, Routledge, 1989.
4 P. Bobbitt, *The Sword of Achilles*, London, Allen Lane, 2002.
5 See, among many others, A. Vincent and R. Plant, *Philosophy, Politics and Citizenship*, Oxford, Basil Blackwell, 1984.
6 Ibid., Chapter 4.
7 J. Rawls, *A Theory of Justice*, Boston, Harvard University Press, 1972.
8 L. Mead, *Beyond Entitlement*, New York, The Free Press, 1986.
9 C. Murray, *In Pursuit of Happiness and Good Government*, New York, Simon and Schuster, 1988.
10 C. A. R. Crosland, *The Future of Socialism*, London, Jonathan Cape, 1956, and *Social Democracy in Europe*, London, The Fabian Society, 1975.
11 See K. Joseph, *Stranded on the Middle Ground*.
12 R. Nozick, *Anarchy, State and Utopia*, Oxford, Basil Blackwell, 1974.

Re-Stating Politics, Re-Politicising the State: Neo-liberalism, Economic Imperatives and the Rise of the Competition State

COLIN HAY

IF SUSTAINED and systematic academic analysis were an index of real-world significance, then the state really would be in trouble. Conversely, were the real-world significance of the state reflected in sustained and systematic academic analysis, all political analysts would be state theorists and the notion of the inexorable demise of the state would long since have been exposed for the myth that it so clearly is. Indeed, no extensive training in the often dense and esoteric language of state theory is required to appreciate the extent of the disparity between, on the one hand, the dominant stylised account of the state's inexorable demise at the hands of globalisation and, on the other, evidence of the state's continued vitality. For, despite the rhetoric, there is scant evidence for the crisis of the nation-state so freely and loosely invoked, as even the crudest of aggregate data reveals. State expenditure as a percentage of GDP in the most open of economies is not significantly lower than that at its high point in the mid-1980s (see Figure 1). Moreover, the correlations between state expenditure and both economic openness and GDP have, if anything, strengthened over the 'era of globalisation'. That such a disparity between rhetoric and reality should continue to exist is surely an indication of both the lack of interest in, and poverty of, contemporary state theory.

The absence of sustained reflection on the contemporary character of the liberal democratic state is all the more remarkable given the proliferation of studies pointing to the decisive role that, variously, globalisation, regionalisation, post-industrialisation and even post-modernisation (whatever that is) have had, or are in the process of having, on its developmental trajectory. Yet all too frequently such debates, as in the case of the globalisation controversy, concentrate almost exclusively on the independent variable, as claim and counterclaim are traded on the extent and indeed the 'reality' of the explanatory variable in question and the degree to which mechanisms of enforced state retrenchment might plausibly be attributed to it. Yet, however intense and protracted the exchanges provoked, the developmental trajectory of actually existing states themselves has remained almost wholly absent from the discussion. This is a depressing state of affairs and is perhaps indicative of a broader crisis if not of the state itself, then certainly of our thinking about it.

 Published by Blackwell Publishing Ltd, 9600 Garsington Road, Oxford OX4 2DQ, UK and 350 Main Street, Malden, MA 02148, USA

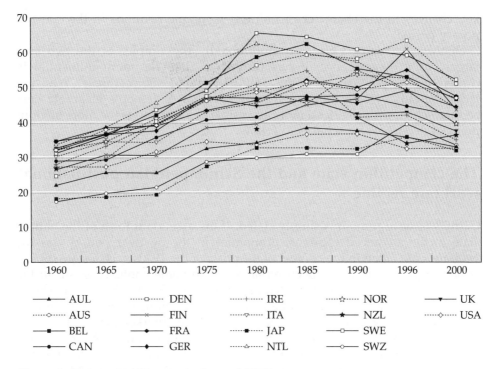

Figure 1: State expenditure as a share of GDP
Source: calculated from OECD, *Economic Outlook*, various years

There are, of course, exceptions to any general rule—and it is with those exceptions that this chapter is principally concerned. Chief amongst these are two ostensibly similar accounts of the developmental trajectory of the nation-state in the advanced capitalist economies since the 1970s. These are Philip G. Cerny's account of the rise of the 'competition state' and Bob Jessop's somewhat more cumbersome account of the emergence of the 'Schumpeterian post-national workfare regime'.[1] Both are distinctive in the context of the existing literature in offering a *positive* account and characterisation of the contemporary state form. Moreover, there are a number of other similarities. Both rely upon a punctuated conception of the developmental trajectory of the nation-state in the postwar period; both identify the cathartic crisis of the 1970s as the moment of punctuation; both stress similarities in the trajectories of the advanced capitalist economies and their associated state regimes at the same point in time at the expense of emphasising variation between cases; both identify the demise of the (Keynesian) welfare state and the rise of the (Schumpeterian) competition state; and both identify exogenous and largely economic pressures for reform, seeing only a limited role for mediating political and ideational variables. Finally, both provide supremely well observed, yet nonetheless general, elegant and parsimonious accounts of key changes in the character of political-economic relations in the contemporary period.

Of these accounts, Cerny's is undoubtedly the simpler of the two and, largely as a consequence, it has proved to date far more influential in contemporary political economy and in cognate subject areas. Whilst it lacks the subtlety, flexibility and sophistication of Jessop's elaborate conceptual schema, it provides a more accessible account and is the more obvious point of departure for what is to follow.

The competition state and the Schumpeterian post-national workfare regime

Cerny's basic argument is simply stated. If the ascendant form of the nation-state in the advanced capitalist economies in the postwar period was the 'welfare state', then in the context of the crisis of the 1970s such a state regime is no longer viable. It has been replaced, or in some contexts is still in the process of being replaced, by the 'competition state'. Where the welfare state's principal priority was the promotion of the welfare of its citizens through the insulation of 'key elements of economic life from market forces', the competition state's principal strategy is one of 'marketisation in order to make economic activities located within the national territory . . . more competitive in international and transnational terms'.[2] Social munificence has been subordinated to perceived economic necessity as the heightened competition engendered by increased capital mobility in an era of globalisation has exposed the welfare state as a somewhat indulgent luxury of a bygone era. All aspects of state policy are essentially exposed, in an era of heightened capital mobility, to an exacting and exhaustive competitive audit at the hands of globalisation. As Cerny explains, diverse models of state intervention are feasible 'only where they constitute relatively efficient alternative modes of adaptation to economic and political globalisation . . . pressures for homogenisation are likely to continue to erode those different models where they prove economically inefficient in world markets'.[3] The result is a new state regime, the competition state, characterised, variously, by: (i) its 'residual' nature (certainly when compared to its welfare state predecessor); (ii) its shift from macroeconomic to microeconomic modes of intervention; (iii) its attempts to promote flexibility and adaptive responses to changing competitive conditions; (iv) its internalisation of the mantras of 'neo-liberal monetarism' with an attendant macroeconomic emphasis upon the control of inflation; and (v) its indirect promotion of welfare (only) through the positive externalities of enterprise, innovation and profitability.[4]

Though the terminology is only partially conserved, Jessop's account is ostensibly similar. However, the often subtle differences are in fact highly significant. For the nuance, subtlety and precision that comes with the caveats, qualifications and conditionalities that litter *The Future of the Capitalist*

State elevate it above the stylish but stylistic parsimony that provides the simple appeal of Cerny's far more accessible account. Limits of space prevent a detailed elaboration of Jessop's thesis. It is nonetheless instructive to identify a few key points of difference.

- For Jessop it is not globalisation but the (putative) shift from Fordism to post-Fordism as a regime of accumulation with an attendant mode of regulation that precipitates the need for the transcendence of the (Keynesian) welfare state.
- The emergent Schumpeterian post-national workfare regime (SPWR) that ('tendentially') replaces the Keynesian welfare national state (KWNS) is still very much in the process of emergence.
- Jessop allows for, and indeed details at some length, possible variations in the form of both the KWNS and the SPWR, differentiating in so doing far more clearly than Cerny between contingent political dynamics (such as neo-liberalisation) and the more necessitarian economic logic underlying the emergence of the SPWR.
- Jessop, unlike Cerny, does make reference (albeit only in passing) to the possibility of alternative state forms to the SPWR that are compatible, in the present context (that is, an emergent post-Fordism), with the expanded reproduction of capital.

Despite these important differences, however, it is what these accounts share that distinguishes them from the vast majority of the existing literature. And, indeed, it is in what they share that the principal problems with these two accounts lie. Space does not permit a detailed review and critical assessment of these important attempts to breathe new life into the attempts to develop a positive theory of the contemporary state. Instead, I point to a series of potential limitations of accounts of this type, assessing the extent to which each might be seen to apply to Cerny and Jessop's variants of the 'competition state' thesis. My remarks take the form of a series of separable, but closely related, critical but sympathetic observations. I conclude by suggesting the need to re-politicise the process of state transformation that is well described, but inadequately explained, by both Cerny and Jessop.

Description or explanation?

A first issue which immediately strikes the reader of this literature is the status of the account of the development of the state in the postwar period that is offered. It is never very clear, in either Cerny or Jessop, whether (1) the account of the emergence of the competition state is intended merely as an abstracted redescription of an observed and exhibited empirical regularity (welfare-state-like entities are being replaced by competition-state-like entities), or (2) the intention is to account for the *logic* and/or *necessity* of that transition, or indeed (3) the intention is to *explain* the emergence of competition-state-like entities as and where they appear.

There is a considerable degree of confusion and conflation in both accounts. At times, especially in Jessop's work, the 'tendential' emergence of the competition state/SPWR is presented as a contingent outcome of a variety of complex and case-specific interactions that are not, by and large, the subject of the narrative itself. Yet on other occasions, and more consistently in the work of Cerny, the transition from the welfare state to the competition state is presented both as a necessity and as the dependent variable to be explained. This is more problematic. For there is something of a tendency to extrapolate from ongoing developments to provide an account of the (emergent) competition-state-like form which is then, retroductively, presented as the only possible response to the crisis of the old regime. The clear danger in this is that the contingent politics, say, of neo-liberalism is presented as a necessary adaptation, imposed upon unwitting states by an almost natural process of competitive selection, to the external economic environment. This tendency is especially acute in Cerny's account of the competition state, though it is by no means entirely avoided by Jessop either. The result is an inadvertent form of neo-liberal apologism which both naturalises and seemingly necessitates whatever political processes throw up.

Functional or functionalist?

This immediately suggests a second and closely related issue—the functional and (possibly) functionalist character of both accounts. As befits its regulation theoretical inspiration, much of Jessop's analysis is couched in functional and economic terms. The SPWR is likely to emerge, to the extent that it does emerge, in economies previously embedded in the circuits (immediate and extended) of Atlantic Fordism in so far as it is capable of stabilising, consolidating and providing the expanded conditions of reproduction of an after-Fordist regime of accumulation. This allows Jessop to speak of, and to conduct much of his analysis in terms of, the ideal-typical form and function of the state for capital accumulation. Cerny's emphasis upon the selection of economically efficient outcomes in a context characterised by heightened competition between economies serves a very similar role. The competition state is likely to emerge, to the extent that it does emerge, in so far as it is capable of internalising the competitive imperatives imposed upon the state in an era of globalisation. Functionality is, once again, selected for.

Now, to be clear, this is not, strictly speaking, functional*ist* if one accepts that the appeal to such functional language is not part and parcel of an attempt to fashion an *explanation* of the developmental trajectory of the state form. Yet some caution is here required. Two points might here be noted.

First, as already suggested, it is not at all clear that Cerny's and Jessop's accounts are not intended as explanatory. What is clear, however, is that to the extent that an explanation of the tendential transition is proffered it is one that is couched in functional terms and hence is functionalist. Whilst this functionalism might be regarded as defensible (in its heuristic value, for instance) at such a high plain of theoretical abstraction, it is unlikely to be to everyone's taste and it is not adequately defended by either author.

Second, even if regarded as of purely heuristic interest and as non-explanatory in content or design, the depiction/derivation of the competition state/SPWR tends to assume that demonstrable economic efficiency/functionality is the key to understanding the replacement of one regime of the capitalist state by another. In other words, for the SPWR to be a credible successor to the KWNS it must contribute towards a resolution of the underlying ('real' as distinct from 'narrated') crisis of Atlantic Fordism. Similarly, for the competition state to be a credible successor to the welfare state it must demonstrate itself functional, where the welfare state was not, in a context characterised by capital mobility and heightened competition between national economies. Yet, as the more detailed and concrete analysis of specific state level developments makes very clear (and as Jessop himself seems to concede at various points) this is dubious. For if, as Jessop acknowledges, it is as solutions to narrated not actual crises that new regimes are legitimated and constituted, then what is to ensure the favourable and functional 'fix' that both authors assume? No compelling mechanism is presented.

A process without a political subject?

By virtue of its privileging of the economic and its exploration of the degree to which the institutional form of the state may prove functional or dysfunctional for the expanded reproduction of capital, the 'competition state thesis' is starkly apolitical. Remarkably, virtually no mention is made in either account of political parties at all, nor of the implications of the putative transition to the competition state/SPWR for the more or less democratic character of economic governance in contemporary societies.[5] Moreover, where—as in Jessop's work—a range of political variables are considered, such factors are accorded only a limited and second-order relevance; indeed, they are generally seen to be operative only at rather lower orders of theoretical abstraction than those with which Jessop's analysis is principally concerned. Partly as a consequence, the 'competition state thesis' is never defended against obvious contenders which are rather more political in nature and which would seem at least equally consistent both with the empirical record and Cerny's and Jessop's stylised presentation of it.

Particularly notable here is the neo-liberalisation thesis (which might take a variety of rather different forms). To be fair to him, Jessop, unlike Cerny, is in fact very clear about the extent to which neo-liberalism has risen, as it were, from the ashes of actually existing Fordism to provide the dominant inflection to the emergent competition state/SPWR. Indeed, he develops a quite credible theory of neo-liberal diffusion, emphasising in particular the role of international institutions in the promotion of neo-liberal 'solutions' to narrated crises.[6] Given, as Jessop freely admits, the uneven character of the tendential development of the SPWR (a point to which we return), is it not then equally plausible to suggest that what we have experienced since the 1970s is a gradual process, albeit again one that is unevenly developed, of neo-liberalisation in response to a variety of perceived, manufactured and genuine crises of extant political-economic regimes?

Such a characterisation of the developing political economy of advanced capitalism has a variety of potential advantages to that proposed by either Cerny or Jessop. Amongst these might be included the following: (i) it requires no necessary appeal to functional logics; (ii) it restores actors to what might otherwise seem a rather agentless process without a subject; (iii) arguably, it can account with rather greater facility for the very different timings of the reform process in different contexts (from the late 1970s in Britain to the 1990s in some Nordic contexts); and (iv) it is rather more consistent with Jessop's own argument that responses are made not to crises *per se* but to their often politically motivated construction *as* crises. Finally, it implies the possibility that the dynamics described by both authors might be held to account democratically and might, indeed, be (or become) subject to political deliberation. For critical political analysts this final point is likely to prove a most attractive competitive advantage.

Whether, in the end, this is a credible alternative thesis is not really the point and certainly cannot be adjudicated here. The point is that if alternatives can be posited which are rather more political and contingent in character (and this is by no means the only one), then they need to be interrogated and dismissed before we settle for the starkly apolitical character of the competition state thesis. Otherwise there is a clear danger, once again, that a highly contingent and political process of neo-liberalisation is mistaken for a simple internalisation of externally imposed and non-negotiable economic imperatives.

Variant forms of state regime

A fourth set of issues relates to the possibility of variant forms of the ascendant state regime at a given point in time. The issue is raised directly by Jessop's account of institutional variation in the form of the KWNS, the SPWR.[7] It is, in fact, rather less relevant to Cerny's more stylised account, which gives little indication that the ascendant state regime (whether welfare state or competition state) may come in variant forms.[8] However, much of the following argument might easily be extended to the work of Cerny.

The key question here is simply stated: given the existence of very significant deviations between the ideal-typical presentation of the KWNS and the SPWR on the one hand, and 'actually existing' cases on the other, what is the utility of presenting an account of the development of the capitalist state form at such a high plain of theoretical abstraction and generality? In other words, if the state in Canada for much of the postwar period lacked many of the distinctive institutional features of a KWNS and is now far from self-evidently in the process of becoming a Schumpeterian competition state, far less an SPWR, then what greater analytical purchase is offered to analysts of Canadian political economy by presenting the development of the Canadian state in such terms?

The same point might be made of just about every case that Jessop's schema seems intended to encompass: from the United States (hardly an archetypal KWNS) to the Nordic countries (which, however archetypally Keynesian and welfarist, have been characterised for a very long time by both high levels of economic openness and active labour market regimes and which arguably only underwent a crisis in the 1990s for reasons which seem to have nothing to do with the transition from actually existing Fordism to after-Fordism). Restated in more general terms, if a specific regime only loosely resembled a KWNS in the 'golden age' of Fordist ascendancy and now bears only a scratchy resemblance to an emergent SPWR, then why would one expect this stylised and self-confessedly ideal-typical narrative to capture the essence of the transition in question, far less to provide concepts capable of illuminating the complex concreteness of that transition? What is it that makes Jessop believe that the determinants of developmental trajectories such as this are operative at such high levels of theoretical abstraction?

Jessop does deal with the general if not the specific issue in passing, but he seems to regard as largely self-evident the value to be gained by constructing a stylised narrative of the evolution of the capitalist state in terms of: (1) the transition from KWNS to SPWR; and (2) the 'structural coupling' of such evolving state regimes to the development of post-Fordism in and through the crisis of Fordism. As he states, 'the general and widespread nature of the changes involved in the tendential emergence of the SPWR suggests that the primary causes of this transition should be sought in general and widespread features of the post-war political economy since the 1970s and 1980s'.[9] This is illuminating and problematic in equal measure. First, it implies, contrary to claims made elsewhere in the text, that the analysis he presents is indeed intended to be causal/explanatory rather than merely an exercise in abstracted redescription, characterisation and classification. Second, and of more immediate relevance, there is a potential circularity here. Put bluntly, Jessop is in danger of assuming that which he must demonstrate. For if the tendential emergence of the SPWR is assumed, then of course it must be explained, and if it is assumed to emerge consistently from the KWNS, then of course it is plausible to look for a common account of the observed transition. But that is precisely the issue that is at stake here; and, moreover, it is an issue that Jessop's own differentiation amongst KWNSs and SPWRs serves to pose as the issue at stake! Quite simply, is the degree of variation observed by Jessop amongst KWNS-like and SPWR-like entities consistent with the identification of a generic (and largely unspecified) mechanism affecting the transition from one to the other? And if a common explanation for ostensibly similar developmental trajectories is to be sought, why not consider some of the obvious contending accounts—such as the rise and diffusion of neo-liberalism? The fact that regimes can be described, to a greater or lesser extent, in KWNS or SPWR terms, need not imply that their development is best (or even adequately) captured in terms of a stylised account of the transition from one to the other.

Whilst the analytical utility of such a stylised narrative can certainly be defended, and the breadth and diversity of the evidence that Jessop and Cerny are able to enlist in support of their case provides at least an implicit defence of that utility, such a defence is far from self-evident and remains to be spelt out.

Finally, there is a certain unevenness in Jessop's treatment of the KWNS and the SPWR. For whereas the former seems, to him at least, consistent with a multitude of welfare regime types (six are specified) and a number of modes of economic governance (four are specified), the latter is not dissected or 'adjectivally enhanced' to anything like the same extent; nor are the developmental trajectories of different welfare regime type-economic governance mixes mapped onto specific variants of the SPWR. Indeed, Jessop classifies Schumpeterian competition states and SPWRs only in terms of their neo-liberal, neo-corporatist, neo-communitarian or neo-statist character, whilst indicating that these are by no means mutually exclusive.[10] It would seem that a great diversity of KWNS-like regimes and/or functional equivalents are in the process of being squeezed in a rather less flexible SPWR box, where each will be governed through a combination of neo-liberal, neo-statist, neo-communitarian and neo-corporatist modes of economic governance. All of this suggests the potential utility of exploring further internal classifications of the SPWR and then looking for family resemblances amongst the developmental trajectories of most similar and, indeed, most different KWNSs. It is surely only if this is done that Jessop can adequately defend the claim that the 'primary causes' of the transitions he describes should indeed 'be sought in general and widespread features of the post-war political economy since the 1970s and 1980s'.[11]

Structure, agency and strategy

A fifth set of concerns relates to the degree of compatibility between, on the one hand, the sophisticated treatments of the structure–agency relationship that both authors are well known for and, on the other, the functional(ist) classification and abstracted redescription of the evolution of the state form in advanced capitalism that both now present.[12]

Given the emphasis placed by both authors in earlier work on the interaction of structure and agency, what is remarkable about the thesis they now advance is that it accords only a most minimal role to specified agents. Both authors here seem to confine themselves largely to a mapping of the strategic terrain on which the developmental tendencies and counter-tendencies of the state are played out. This is a strangely agentless pursuit. And it is somewhat at odds with what many have taken to be the central and defining concern of both structuration theory (in Cerny's case) and the strategic-relational approach (in Jessop's case)—a desire to demonstrate and to reflect theoretically the dynamic interplay between agency and structure, strategy and strategic context.

Sadly, neither author has much to say about strategy or strategic actors, though they certainly have much to contribute to an assessment of the uneven contours of the terrain such actors must negotiate. This is a product no doubt of the simple fact that the ethereal realms of abstraction at which the analysis is for the most part conducted are not densely populated with clearly identifiable actors, strategic or otherwise. Again, it would seem, the choice of such a high degree of abstraction and generality needs to be justified—and may well be incompatible with any attempt to reflect theoretically the view of the structure–agency relationship both authors have elsewhere defended.

Alternatives: improving on perfection?

The rather agentless character of the competition state thesis raises one final and closely related point—the failure to explore systematically the alternatives to the competition state/SPWR. Again, to be fair to him, Jessop is clearly well aware of the issue and, as elsewhere, goes some considerable way towards anticipating this potential avenue of critique. Yet arguably, in so doing, he creates as many problems as he resolves. It is instructive here to consider two comments in particular.

First, whilst acknowledging, really for the first time, that alternatives to the SPWR do exist (or might be posited), Jessop states 'it is not my intention to offer an alternative to the SPWR as it is outlined here as a key element in the mode of regulation of contemporary capitalism, let alone to propose a detailed blueprint for an alternative to capitalism as a mode of production'. He continues: 'such a limited study cannot provide the basis for sketching an alternative, which would need to embrace the entire world market and lifeworld and thus look well beyond the confines of the spatio-temporal matrices with which this work is concerned'.[13] Presumably, this second passage relates more to the difficulties in sketching an alternative mode of production than it does to the question of credible alternatives to the SPWR. For it is difficult to see why it would be necessary to 'embrace the entire world market and the lifeworld' to begin to explore the parameters of political and economic choice within actually existing capitalism. Indeed, surely all that is entailed is a discussion, for instance, of whether the subordination of social policy to (perceived) economic imperatives is itself a necessary correlate of any stable mode of economic growth after Fordism. And it is, in many respects, quite remarkable that Jessop doesn't engage in an analysis of this type. If this workfarist element is not a necessary condition of competitiveness, as I for one would contend, then it is imperative that we consider the alternatives, whatever the inherent difficulties of the exercise.

Jessop concludes his all too brief discussion of alternatives by declaring his hope that 'the modest remarks contained in this work will . . . contribute to the search for alternatives'.[14] This is a particularly intriguing comment, suggesting as it does that alternatives to the SPWR, despite its seeming functionality for post-Fordism, may well be preferable (normatively) to the SPWR itself. Yet hoping that his work might contribute to the search for alternatives may not be sufficient. For, arguably, in presenting the SPWR as the functional correlate of post-Fordism, Jessop may well have served inadvertently to insulate it from the type of critique likely to prompt a discussion of the alternatives. The same might be said of Cerny's account of the competition state, which fails even to acknowledge the possibility of (stable) alternatives in a context of globalisation.

One final concluding comment of Jessop's perhaps serves to reinforce the point. In a self-confessedly audacious aphorism, he summarises the overall argument of the book in the following terms: 'a Schumpeterian post-national workfare regime will provide the best possible—but still imperfect and provisional—spatio-temporal fix for a globalising, knowledge-based, post-Fordist economy'.[15] This is a very telling remark in a number of respects. First, it reminds us that the SPWR, though emergent, has yet to materialise in full. If it does, then one must presume this to be a triumph of capitalism's ability to conjure for itself optimal economic functionality out of the contingencies of political conflict and contestation. That would be some achievement. For quite why we should expect the most economically efficient outcome to manifest itself is, of course, never explained. Second, the precise meaning of the 'best possible' is left ambiguous. Given his earlier remarks one can only presume that the comment is not intended to imply a normative endorsement (for 'best possible' we should not read 'most desirable'). Rather, it seems, 'best possible' means 'economically most functional'. If this is indeed the case, it raises once again the question of why—given what we know about the historical development of actually existing capitalism and the inherently political processes and struggles in and through which state regimes emerge and are replaced—we would expect the best outcome (in whatever sense of the term) to be the most likely outcome.

Finally, we might ask, how do we know this to be the best possible outcome if we have not considered the alternatives?

Conclusion

As the above analysis has hopefully served to indicate, there are striking similarities between Cerny's and Jessop's accounts of the developmental trajectories of advanced liberal democratic states in the postwar period. Moreover, whatever their weaknesses, both perspectives represent major interventions in debates on the past, present and future of the capitalist state. They lay out an agenda for future research and scholarship, present a powerful set of challenges to conventional understandings and provide an important point of departure for all future work in this area. Yet like all classic works of social science, their value lies as much in their ability to provoke debate and discussion as in their substantive contribution, important though that is.

Moreover, like the competition state/SPWR that is its principal focus of analysis, the competition state thesis should be seen as works in progress. As I have sought to demonstrate, it is perhaps more effective in describing the developmental trajectory of the state today than it is at providing an adequate explanation of that trajectory. This, I have argued, is a product of the functional, apolitical and largely agentless nature of the analysis offered—a reflection, in turn, of the high plains of theoretical abstraction and generality at which the thesis operates. If the future of the capitalist state that it depicts is not a very enticing prospect—indeed, if the acceptance of the competition state/SPWR seems at times to herald a worrying capitulation to neo-liberal orthodoxy—then it is crucial that we tease out the contingent nature of the dynamics that Cerny and Jessop describe so well. In order to do so we must descend from the high plains of theoretical abstraction, resist the temptation to functionalist explanation and reanimate contemporary state theory with political actors. In re-stating politics, then, we must also re-politicise the state.

Notes

1 Philip G. Cerny, 'Globalisation and the changing logic of collective action', *International Organization*, 1995, pp. 595–625; 'Paradoxes of the competition state: the dynamics of political globalisation', *Government and Opposition*, 1997, pp. 251–74; Bob Jessop, 'Towards a Schumpeterian workfare state? Preliminary remarks on post-Fordist political economy', *Studies in Political Economy*, 1993, pp. 7–39; *The Future of the Capitalist State*, Cambridge, Polity, 2002.
2 Cerny, 'Paradoxes of the competition state', pp. 258, 259.
3 Cerny, ibid., p. 251.
4 Cerny, 'Globalisation and the changing logic of collective action', pp. 598, 612–13; 'Paradoxes of the competition state', p. 260.
5 There is, in fact, only one exception to this. Cerny points briefly, and in passing, to the 'new and potentially undemocratic role' that the state must increasingly perform in satisfying economic (rather than political) imperatives. Yet sadly this potentially highly significant comment is never developed—presumably because Cerny simply assumes there to be no choice other than the subordination of political priorities and democratic demands to economic imperatives. Cerny, 'Paradoxes of the competition state', p. 258.
6 Jessop, *The Future of the Capitalist State*, p. 132.
7 Jessop, ibid., pp. 58 ff.
8 Though see Cerny, 'Paradoxes of the competition state', pp. 263–8. Here Cerny does acknowledge that the dominant form of the competition state is the 'neoliberal state' (p. 265).
9 Jessop, *The Future of the Capitalist State*, p. 142.
10 Ibid., pp. 259–67.

11 Ibid., p. 142.
12 On the structure–agency relationship, see especially Cerny, *The Changing Architecture of the State*, London, Sage, 1990; Jessop, *The Capitalist State: Putting Capitalist States in Their Place*, Cambridge, Polity, 1990.
13 Jessop, *The Future of the Capitalist State*, p. 247.
14 Ibid., p. 248.
15 Ibid., p. 268.

False Friend: The State and the Public Domain

DAVID MARQUAND

RUNNING through the current debate on the 'reform' of the public services, the level of public spending on those services and the implications of both of these for the Blair government and British social democracy is a tacit assumption which can be traced back to the earliest years of the Fabian tradition. This is that the public domain or public realm—the realm of citizenship, equity and service, where pursuit of the public interest takes precedence over private ties and market transactions—is either coterminous with, or at least guaranteed and protected by, the democratic state. As far back as the *Fabian Essays* of 1889, George Bernard Shaw distilled the essence of this assumption with a characteristic mixture of tendentiousness and brilliance. In the early nineteenth century, he wrote, incompetence and corruption had been 'inherent state qualities, like the acidity of lemons'. But the modern state was a very different animal. The state bureaucracy was recruited on merit, assessed by public examinations; and the government was responsible to the people through democratic elections. (He failed to add that only about 60 per cent of the adult male population had votes.) As a result, socialists had become democrats. But they were democrats of a special kind. Unlike old-fashioned Radicals, who merely wished to pull up aristocratic institutions by the roots, social democrats wished 'through Democracy *to gather the whole people into the State*, so that the State may be trusted with the rent of the country, and finally with the land, the capital and the organization of the national industry' (my italics).[1]

Gathering the whole people into the state was pitching it a little high; and social-democratic rhetoric later became more nuanced. But for more than 100 years, British social democrats viewed the relationship between the state and the public domain through an essentially Shavian prism. Public ownership meant state ownership. The public services were state services. Public servants were state servants. Public goods were delivered by the state, and paid for out of taxation raised by the state. Above all, the public interest was defined by the state, and pursued by agencies of the state. Marxists and quasi-Marxists sometimes suggested that the character, history and inherited values of the British state made it an unsuitable instrument for a socialist or even a social-democratic project; and there are traces of a similar attitude in the writings of R. H. Tawney. But that was not the majority view. Most social democrats took it for granted that the state had been democratised by the extensions of the suffrage which had taken place between 1832 and 1918; and

© The Political Quarterly Publishing Co. Ltd. 2004
Published by Blackwell Publishing Ltd, 9600 Garsington Road, Oxford OX4 2DQ, UK and 350 Main Street, Malden, MA 02148, USA

concluded that democratic citizenship and state intervention were different sides of the same coin.

Here, as elsewhere, New Labour is Old Labour writ small. The Blair governments have abandoned the old social-democratic dream of mastering or transcending capitalism. Nothing could be further from their minds than handing over the nation's land, capital and industry to the state, in the way that Shaw thought inevitable and necessary. Their conception of citizenship is thin and attenuated in comparison with those of erstwhile social-democratic champions, such as Tawney, Evan Durbin and Anthony Crosland. They have taken over the consumerist rhetoric of the Thatcher and Major governments, together with the cult of private-sector managerialism and the vogue for marketisation that it reflects. Yet, in a strange, upside-down way, they have remained faithful to the *étatisme* of the British social-democratic tradition. The public domain of citizenship, equity and service, they assume, is bound to be strengthened if more resources are devoted to the public services, even if they are accompanied by 'reforms' designed to blur the distinction between the public domain and the market domain. All that matters is that the resources should come from the state. Provided they do, it does not matter if the citizen is transmogrified into a customer, and the public services into clones of Sainsbury's or Tesco's. Indeed, it is positively desirable. We all know—don't we?—that nowadays citizens ask for nothing better than to be treated as customers.

The public domain and the public sector

In this essay I shall argue that matters are more complicated; that the public domain goes much wider than the public sector; and that although the state can be, and has sometimes been, its friend, it can also be its enemy. In Britain as in the rest of Europe, the state came before the public domain. Henry VIII, Elizabeth I, Philip II, Francis I and the other leading monarchs of early-modern Europe ruled powerful and imposing states but they did not acknowledge a public interest transcending private interests. Still less did they acknowledge any obligation to pursue it. The 'kingly state', as Philip Bobbitt calls it,[2] was an emanation of the sovereign ('L'état c'est moi', Louis XIV famously declared), not a separate entity standing above both ruler and ruled. More than 300 years later, the totalitarian party-states of the twentieth century were emanations of the party and the Leader. They perverted the service ethic of the public domain into an instrument of party control, and remodelled its practices to fit party imperatives. Both in Hitler's Germany and in Stalin's Soviet Union, in other words, the state effectively destroyed the public domain—not that Tsarist Russia had had much of a public domain before the revolution.

The public domain, as I understand it, depends on public institutions (notably the rule of law), but it is not confined to them. In principle, a large public domain could coexist with a small public sector. There is certainly nothing sacrosanct about the ratio between the two which obtained in mid- and late twentieth century Britain. In earlier periods, the ratio was very different; and there is no reason of principle why it should not be different in future. The growth of the public domain provides one of the central themes of nineteenth-century British history. For most of that period, the public sector grew much more slowly. Government expenditure as a proportion of GNP was lower in 1900 than it had been in 1831, and in absolute terms it did not grow very much until the decade of the 1890s. The state facilitated the growth of the public domain in that crucial period, but with one important exception it did not generate it.

The exception was that, under Gladstone, the reforms in public adminis- tration recommended in the Northcote–Trevelyan Report were put into effect. The cronyism and nepotism that Radicals had excoriated as 'Old Corruption' were swept away. A professional, non-partisan career civil service, recruited by open public examination instead of by patronage, became a fundamental feature of the British state. This was a critically important milestone in the growth of the public domain; and it was the work of a reforming state. Apart from that, however, the chief drivers of the process were the rapidly expanding self-governing professions; local authorities; self-help working- class institutions such as trades unions, friendly societies and cooperatives; private charities; and dissenting chapels. It was in these that the values and practices of citizenship were learned. Most important of all was a slow but far-reaching change in what Gladstone called the 'public conscience'.[3] This certainly impacted on the state, but the state did not impact much on it.

The public domain should not be seen as a 'sector' at all. It is best understood as a dimension of social life, with its own norms and decision rules, cutting across sectoral boundaries: as a set of practices, which can be (and historically have been) carried out by private individuals, private charities and even private firms as well as by public agencies. It is symbio- tically linked to the notion of a public interest, in principle distinct from private interests; central to it are the values of citizenship, equity and service. In it goods are distributed on the basis of need and not of personal ties or access to economic resources. It is a space, protected from the adjacent market and private domains, where strangers encounter each other as equal partners in the common life of the society—a space for forms of human flourishing which cannot be bought in the marketplace or found in the tight-knit community of the clan or family or group of intimates. In it, citizenship rights trump both market power and kinship or neighbourhood bonds; the duties of citizenship take precedence both over market incentives and over private loyalties. The state can snuff out these civic values, but it cannot engender them.

The goods of the public domain include fair trials, welcoming public spaces, free public libraries, subsidised opera, mutual building societies, safe food, the broadcasts of the BBC World Service, the lobbying of Amnesty International, clean water, impartial public administration, disinterested scholarship, blood donors, magistrates, the minimum wage, the Pennine Way, the National Trust and the rulings of the Health and Safety Executive. Some of these are financed by the state, but some are not. Much the same is true of occupations. State servants like policemen, civil servants, judges and soldiers normally belong to the public domain. Foreign exchange dealers, super- market managers, software designers and pop musicians inhabit the market domain. But many occupations cross the frontier between the two. In one optic, barristers are market traders, selling their wares in a highly competitive marketplace, where rents of ability can be very high. But that is not all they are. They also have duties to the court. Their primary duty is to ensure that justice is fairly and impartially administered; and that duty is supposed to override their economic interests. It is not confined to barristers whose fees are paid by the public purse. It applies to wealthy silks with lucrative commercial practices and annual earnings in seven figures as well as to the Rumpoles of the profession who depend on legal aid. Trades unions also sell their wares—or rather their members' wares—in the marketplace. They exist to screw the highest possible price for their members' labour power out of potential purchasers. But in doing this they mitigate what Keynes famously called 'the theory of the economic juggernaut' in the name of the non-market principle of the just price; in doing so they also promote the public good of industrial citizenship. They do not do this at the behest of the state. Frequently, they find themselves ranged against it.

In the days before the 1911 National Insurance Act, most doctors earned their living from privately paid fees. But many doctors adjusted their fee schedules to their patients' ability to pay and they did so because they subscribed, at least to some degree and in some cases, to a public-service ethic. Before universities were funded by the state, academic salaries were paid from the university's fee income. Despite charitable benefactions which financed scholarships for the exceptionally talented, access to a university education was largely confined to those who could pay for it. But academics also adhered (or tried intermittently to adhere) to a public-service ethic which told them to promote the public goods of disinterested learning, a qualified elite and the transmission of high culture to the young. These values decreed a meritocratic examination system and ruled out the sale of degrees. Doctors and academics did not suddenly become part of the public domain when the state began to pay their salaries. They had belonged to it before. Academics at the private University of Buckingham belong to it now. So do hospital consultants whose earnings come partly from private patients and partly from the NHS. What matter are the ethics or ethic that motivate providers, and the institutions and practices that embody and transmit those ethics, not the source of their salaries. Even if they earn their living in a market of some sort, doctors, lawyers, educators, trades union bargainers, architects and engineers are not rationally calculating market actors, behav- ing in accordance with the profit motive—or, at any rate, not solely. At least in principle, they are supposed to abide by an ethic of public service that tells them to pursue the public interest. That ethic operates independently of the state.

Trust, liberty and the British state

The public domain and its practices are also the sources of public trust. As wise economic liberals have always known, markets cannot work properly without trust. Nor, of course, can governments. But the market domain *consumes* trust; it does not produce it. Market actors have to trust each other. If they don't or can't, there is no market; there are only pirates or gangsters, preying on the weak and unwary. In a trustless society, exorbitant transaction costs would make market exchanges unfeasible. Trust can, of course, be produced in the private domain, and in small, face-to-face societies the trust relationships of the private domain may keep transaction costs low enough for markets to emerge. But private trust relationships are, by definition, narrow and introverted. Close-knit Peak District villages, where you are not accepted unless at least one of your grandparents is buried in the churchyard, are not apt to trust strangers. Once market relationships extend beyond the narrow confines of a face-to-face community, public trust is indispensable to them. And public trust, like the public domain itself, is an artefact. It is a by-product of the argument and debate which are part and parcel of the public domain, and of the institutions that embody and transmit its values: an epiphenomenon of the *practice* of citizenship.

For in the public domain market rationality is transcended by a civic rationality which induces trust through a complex process of social learning. But the learning process does not occur spontaneously. It depends on the institutions of the public domain and on the constraints they impose. The market economy depends, among other things, on the rule of law, enforceable contracts, enforceable property rights and an efficient fraud squad—all quintessential products of the public domain. They make it possible for market actors to learn to trust each other after all. And what is true of trust in the marketplace is true more generally. Citizens trust each other because, and to the extent that, they are citizens: because, and to the extent that, they know that public institutions are governed by an ethic of equity and service. If that ceases to be true, if the public domain succumbs to the ever-present threat of invasion by the market and private domains, if justice is on sale or public offices go to kinsfolk or clients, if professionals behave as if they were market traders and nothing else, trust and citizenship are both undermined. A crucial task of the state is to do everything in its power to ensure that this does not happen. It is—or ought to be—the guardian of the public domain. But, as the example of Gladstone shows, a small state, absorbing only a low proportion of GDP, can perform that duty at least as well as a big one.

Less obviously, the goods of the public domain also include liberty—not in the familiar sense of freedom to pursue private interests, but in the classical republican sense of freedom from domination. In the public domain market power is overridden and private clientelism forbidden; citizens bow the knee to nobody. And, in principle at least, republican liberty goes with democratic self-government and state accountability. In the public domain citizens collectively define what the public interest is to be, through struggle, argument, debate and negotiation. If the rulers of the state and the officials who serve them are not accountable to the citizenry and their representatives, the language of the public interest can become a cloak for the private interests of public persons.

A monarchical state

Against that background, the traditional social-democratic vision of the British state looks astonishingly naïve. In a host of ways, the British state is still, as it always has been, monarchical. Gladstone's reforms cleaned up the patronage-infested state of the eighteenth and early nineteenth centuries, but they were not intended to realise a vision of republican liberty and did not do so. At the core of British government lay a tradition of autonomous executive power, going back to the eighteenth century and perhaps even to royalist apologists at the start of the English Civil War. The monarch's prerogative powers had passed to the Queen's ministers, not to Parliament or the people; and they were still essentially monarchical in character. The Northcote–Trevelyan inspired reforms were explicitly intended to reserve the highest posts in the new, patronage-free bureaucracy to a small elite drawn over-whelming from the two ancient universities. Despite his deepening faith in the civic potential of the masses, Gladstone was, in this sense, a quintessential Whig, whose purpose was to repair and even, if necessary, to reconstruct an ancient building, not to build a new one. The new, corruption-free Glad-stonian state was a cleaned-up version of the old state. The new groups admitted to the franchise were admitted only because it was assumed that they had the capacity to be socialised into the values and *mores* of the existing regime. With only a handful of exceptions, the new men who arrived little by little in the House of Commons were indeed socialised into them. In a mordant phrase, J. G. A. Pocock once said that when democratization came to Britain, it 'arrived by the medieval technique of expanding the king-in-parliament to include new categories of counsellors and representatives'.[4] This almost instinctive medievalism was Gladstone's improbable lodestar.

Exit, Voice and state intervention

What was true of the Gladstonian state was equally true of the interventionist, welfare state that grew up in Britain during the first half of the last century. Under the postwar Labour government, in particular, social citizenship made great advances. Political citizenship became 'thinner' and more passive. The monarchical Gladstonian state had become incomparably bigger, but it was still monarchical; thanks to the increased size and complexity of government and the growth of a disciplined party system, the ministers and officials at the head of it were, in practice, less accountable to Parliament and the public than they had been 70 years before. One of the by-products of the Beveridgean and Keynesian revolutions, moreover, was a much more centralised polity and a much more powerful state. The once-vigorous local government sector, which had been one of the drivers of the expanding public domain of the nineteenth century, now saw its wings severely clipped. The nationalisation of the public utilities—electricity and gas in particular—cut heavily into the autonomy of the local authorities which had owned substantial portions of both. Power was transferred from elected councillors, relatively close to the communities for which they spoke, to remote authorities only dubiously accountable to elected persons of any sort.

The implications go wide. Accountability in the market domain comes through Exit and the threat of Exit. That is how producers are made accountable to consumers, and how consumers ensure that they are not exploited by market power or vested interests. In the public domain, however, accountability through Exit is, by definition, not available. The relationships of the public domain are necessarily long term. The loyalties which are fundamental to it could not take root in, and would not survive, a regime of Exit. It follows that, in the public domain, accountability can come only through Voice—in other words through argument, discussion, debate and democratic engagement. But the pre-democratic, monarchical traditions of the British state have always been in tension with the need for social spaces in which these can flourish. These traditions survived the successive extensions of the suffrage that marked the nineteenth century, and the growth in the role and size of the state that marked the first half of the twentieth. They still survive today.

Centralisation and marketisation

In the last quarter of a century, the tension between monarchical tradition and the requirements of Voice has become far more acute. Part of the explanation lies in the privatisation of political leadership. In the early-modern period, the distinction between the monarch as private person and the monarch as the embodiment of public power did not exist. Henry VIII's marital adventures had direct and, as it turned out, lasting consequences for the English state and church because monarch and man were the same. In our time, the same is beginning to be true of the elective monarch, whether President or Prime Minister, who heads the state machine. Increasingly, we demand of our rulers not just that they be competent in ruling, but that they be authentic human beings as well: that they appear before us unmasked, without disguises, in all their vulnerable humanity. Indeed, we pay more attention to their private selves—or, rather, to what they eagerly display to us as their private selves—than to their public conduct. (With extraordinary perversity, we also demand that the private behaviour of our leaders should conform to public norms: that the unmasked, authentic ruler should, in private, live up to exemplary standards which other private persons are not expected to observe. The extraordinary mixture of farce, hysteria and religiosity that followed the revelation of Bill Clinton's affair with Monica Lewinsky is only one example of the consequences.)

With all this has come a new version of the politics of connection and patronage which the Gladstonian reformers drove out. Increasingly, the Prime Minister's office in Downing Street Britain resembles a Renaissance court. Of course, this has always been true in some degree. Court politics are a feature of political life in all societies at all times. (They were more than usually prominent during the wartime premierships of Lloyd George and Churchill.) But in peacetime Britain, court politics were comparatively unobtrusive until the second half of the last century. They began to obtrude during the Wilson governments of the 1960s, when the No. 10 'kitchen cabinet' was notorious—more notorious, perhaps, than its influence on policy merited. In the 1970s, they were institutionalised by the creation of a Policy Unit of personal appointees to advise the Prime Minister and by the emergence of a network of ministerial 'special advisers', who also owed their posts to the personal favour of their bosses. Under Thatcher and far more under Blair, the process has accelerated. Increasingly, what counts is access to the monarch's person, just as it did under Henry VIII and Louis XIV. And access is increasingly divorced from public roles. Under Blair, Peter Mandelson, Alastair Campbell, Jonathan Powell, young and unheard of members of the Policy Unit, Cabinet ministers and long-serving senior civil servants jostle for the prince's ear as their forerunners jostled in the courts of early-modern times.

For all practical purposes, the Northcote–Trevelyan doctrine that public administration should be conducted by a disinterested, non-partisan civil service, with a professional ethic and career paths protected from political interference, has been jettisoned. The politically appointed advisers I mentioned a moment ago proliferate, particularly at the apex of government in 10 Downing Street. (Where John Major's government made do with thirty-eight, Blair's first government had seventy-four.) More significant than the increase in their numbers is the enhancement of their roles, and the consequent blurring of the old distinction between professional public servants and ministerial appointees. Herein lies the real significance of the Hutton Inquiry. It showed that the Prime Minister's personal aides were, in effect, vetting the findings of the intelligence professionals; and that the roles of Sir John Scarlett, the professional who chaired the Joint Intelligence Committee, and Alastair Campbell, the Prime Minister's personally appointed Director of Communications, had become almost indistinguishable.

This blurring of roles has not been confined to highly charged issues such as those raised by David Kelly's suicide. On some quite mundane issues, members of the Prime Minister's Policy Unit, also unelected, are probably as influential as Cabinet ministers, nominally answerable to the House of Commons. One of the first things Blair did when he entered office was to give Alastair Campbell, and his chief of staff, Jonathan Powell, authority over civil servants. (Parliament had no say in this portentous change in Britain's unwritten constitution, since it was made by Orders in Council, in other words by using the royal prerogative.) Many top civil service posts have been filled by outsiders from the corporate sector. These new entrants may widen the gene pool of Whitehall, but by definition they not been socialised into the professional ethic of the career civil service of the past. They are inherently more dependent on ministerial favour than old-style civil servants used to be, and less eager to preserve the boundaries between the public and market domains: they would not have been recruited in the first place if those boundaries had remained inviolate.

More important than any of this is the conversion of the monarchical state into an agent of marketisation. The process began under Thatcher, when ministers embarked on an extraordinary project of socio-moral engineering, designed to implant what they called an 'enterprise culture' in presumably unenterprising British hearts and minds. The story is well known, and there is no need to recount it here. What matters for the purposes of this essay is that the core executive at the heart of the state set itself, quite deliberately, to force the public services and the professionals who staffed them into a market mould. Three aspects of a complex and sometimes messy story stand out. The most obvious (and in some ways the most important) was linguistic. The language of service and citizenship was subtly transformed into a language of buyers and sellers. Doctors became 'purchasers' and hospitals 'providers'. Passengers became 'customers'. Academics boasted of being 'entrepreneurial'. Funding cuts became 'efficiency gains'. In the University of Salford, where I worked throughout the Thatcher years, departmental chairmen became 'line managers'. The second aspect was a self-reinforcing audit explosion, based on the implicit assumption that the professional ethic was a con; that professionals could not be trusted to deliver unless they were kept on their toes by repeated externally imposed targets and assessments. The third was a marked acceleration in the process of centralisation which had been a *leitmotiv* of British government, certainly since the Second World War and perhaps since the First. Behind all this lay two crucial assumptions, both antithetical to the very notion of the public domain and to the civic ideal of engagement and debate that lies at its heart. The first was that the public services could and should behave as though they were private firms. The second was that the central state had both the right and the duty to remodel civil society, by *fiat* from the top.

In essentials, Blair has followed where Thatcher led. His biggest departure from the previous regime is a series of constitutional changes, notably the incorporation of the European Human Rights Convention into British law, and devolution in Scotland and Wales. These have imposed new limits on the power of the central state, and the second has also created new opportunities for civic engagement. Despite recent talk of a 'new localism', however, the Blair governments have tightened central control over local government as enthusiastically as their predecessors did. There is no sign that Blair and his colleagues dispute their predecessors' assumption that the private corporate sector offers the sole model for the efficient management of public services. The trust-denying audit explosion, which the Thatcher governments helped to ignite, still continues. In universities, schools, hospitals and social service departments, performance indicators, league tables and centrally imposed targets still undermine professional autonomy and narrow the scope for professional judgement. Constitutional reform has left the essentials of Britain's *ancien regime* in place, at least in England. Civil servants are still servants of the Crown, not of Parliament or the public. Most of the Crown's extensive prerogative powers are still at the disposal of the government of the day. The monarchical state and the public domain have always been uneasy bedfellows. Under Blair as under Thatcher, the former now seems bent on undermining the latter. The result is a spreading culture of distrust.

Implications

The most obvious implication is that the public domain, pre-eminently an invention of the Victorian age, should now be reinvented. Another is that a necessary (though not sufficient) condition of its reinvention is the dis-invention of the monarchical state. First steps towards this would have to include a civil service act, making civil servants servants of Parliament instead of the Crown, and imposing strict limits on the number of posts that can be filled by ministerial patronage; the virtual abolition of the Royal Prerogative; an elected second Chamber; proportional representation in elections to the House of Commons; and a sustained programme to strengthen local government and protect it from the inevitable incursions of the centre.

However, reforms of this sort—though eminently desirable in themselves—will not get far without two more fundamental changes in the values and assumptions which social democrats have taken for granted for more than a century. The first has to do with the ingrained *étatisme* which is part of the warp and woof of the mainstream social-democratic tradition. In this essay I have so far criticised the shortcomings of the British state—its monarchical traditions and structures; its propensity for centralisation; its fatal lack of accountability—and the reforms I listed a moment ago are intended to deal with these. But a deeper and more general critique is needed as well. The British state is a peculiarly gross example of the dangers of *étatisme*, but it is the role of the state as such, not of the British state in particular, that social democrats now need to question. The values of republican liberty and civic engagement wither and die unless they are *practised*; and they are far easier to practise in the intermediate institutions of civil society than in the institutions of the central state. This means that the state's role *vis-à-vis* the public domain of citizenship and service is bound to be negative rather than positive. It can, and should, protect the sites of civic engagement from invasion by the market domain, but it cannot easily create new sites. I mentioned earlier that a range of institutions standing between the individual and the central state—local authorities, trades unions, professional bodies, charities, friendly societies, self-governing nonconformist chapels and the like—were the pacemakers of the public domain in Victorian Britain. One of the reasons is that they were also schools of citizenship, in a sense that could never have been true of the central state itself. Political and constitutional reform, in short, is not enough. If the public domain is to recover, the left will have to retrieve the pluralist, non-state, sometimes even anti-state themes that sounded quite loudly in the early years of the last century, only to be drowned out after the First World War. The young G. D. H. Cole, perhaps the young Harold Laski and certainly the mature John Stuart Mill have more to contribute to the social democracy of the twenty-first century than Evan Durbin or Anthony Crosland.

The second fundamental change is closely related to the first. *Étatisme* has gone hand in hand with a profoundly teleological conception of history, modernity and the future. Social democrats have been for 'progress' and for 'modernisation'. They have taken it for granted that history moved in a determinate, knowable direction; that they knew what the direction was; that a better, progressive, socialist or social-democratic future would sooner or later come to pass; and that, by virtue of their superior knowledge of the dynamics of change, they had a duty to overcome the obstacles to that better future. This was most obviously true of Marxist-Leninists, but—albeit less flagrantly—it was also true of dyed-in-the-wool social democrats, to whom Marxist-Leninism was anathema. Sidney Webb spoke glowingly of 'the inevitability of gradualness'; Ramsay MacDonald thought social change was an essentially biological process, in which advanced forms (that is, socialism) would gradually supersede backward ones (capitalism).

Here too New Labour is Old Labour writ small. Its conception of social change is as teleological as that of earlier generations of social democrats; but its teleology points away from social democracy as traditionally understood, not towards it. 'New, new, new', Tony Blair told a meeting of European socialist leaders in a characteristic outburst, shortly after entering office, 'everything is new'.[5] This has been the *leitmotiv* of countless government pronouncements. The world is new, ministers insist, modernity is unproblematic and the path to the future is linear. There is one modern condition, which only the 'forces of conservatism' resist. Change is an irresistible force, operating independently of human agency. Political and ideological arguments for the Third Way are unnecessary. It does not have to be defended against alternative visions of the future, based on different ideological premises. There is only one future. The choices it poses are technical, not moral or political. Its advent is inexorable and unstoppable. From it, there is no hiding place: in it, no room for local ways of life with which its imperatives are in conflict. To think otherwise is to succumb to sentimentality or nostalgia.

The 'revolution of change', of which Tony Blair spoke, is a kind of treadmill from which we cannot dismount.

It is nonsense, of course. The only certainty about the future is that it will be different from the present, in ways we cannot predict. Modernity has many faces. Which is more modern? GM food or organic farming? Nuclear power or wind power? Motorways or bicycle lanes? A deregulated labour market or a 35-hour week? Suburban shopping malls or revitalised city centres? Only half-concealed by the teleology of modernisation is the assumption that the agenda of the dominant players in the global marketplace is, by definition, modern and that the only motive for seeking an alternative is fear of change. A related assumption is that the American model of capitalism is the wave of the future, and that all other models have been, or soon will be, superseded. Both assumptions are problematic and contestable.

In the political sphere, at any rate, two paradigms of modernity are now in contest. One is essentially managerial. It is the paradigm of enlightened—or at least successful—modern corporations. It is about control, assessment, audit, measurement, surveillance. Those who hold it talk the language of teamwork, consultation, even decentralisation. But tasks are set at the top, not negotiated with those at the bottom; the parameters of consultation are defined at the top as well. In a profound sense, it is a paradigm of distrust. Those who are called upon to discharge tasks cannot be trusted by those who decide what the tasks are to be; even the taskmasters cannot be trusted by their peers. The second paradigm is pluralistic. It values autonomy, creativity and diversity. It is a paradigm of negotiation and mutual learning. Its exponents are instinctively suspicious of central control, and seek checks and balances to restrain central power. For them, change—worthwhile and lasting change, at any rate—comes from the bottom up. Albeit haltingly and uncertainly, New Labour's early constitutional reforms sprang from the second paradigm. Its political economy springs from the first. That contradiction lies at the heart of its failure to break away from its predecessors' approach to the public domain. Here, above all, is where change is needed.

Notes

1 George Bernard Shaw, 'The transition to Social Democracy', in Asa Briggs (ed.), *Fabian Essays*, London, George Allen and Unwin, 1962 edition, p. 216.
2 Philip Bobbitt, *The Shield of Achilles: War, Peace and the Course of History*, London, Penguin Books, 2003, pp. 95–143.
3 H. C. G. Matthew, *Gladstone 1875–1898*, Oxford, Clarendon Press, 1995, p. 85.
4 J. G. A. Pocock, *The Machiavellian Moment: Florentine Political Thought and the Atlantic Political Tradition*, Princeton, Princeton University Press, 1975, p. 547
5 Quoted in Stephen Driver and Luke Martell, *New Labour: Politics after Thatcherism*, Cambridge, Polity, 1998, p. 41.

Leviathan Lite

DAVID WALKER

THE FOREIGNNESS of that word 'state' is indicative. The British state lies in shards. Public powers are fragmented. A precondition for success in a number of policy areas is a new concept of statehood. The public sector in each of the UK's countries needs to be rebranded and the state's staff trained together in new 'comprehensives'—if progressive government is to have half a chance . . .

Introduction

Here are two vignettes. Near his retirement, I interviewed the chairman of the board of Inland Revenue, Sir Nick Montagu. That 'Nick' is his. In this corner of the state, wherever authority comes from, it does not any longer rely on formality of address. Overlooking Waterloo Bridge and the South Bank, great memorials to the state as cause of expanded public amenity, he occupies a large corner office in Somerset House. That name, the Lord Protector's, reminds us of long continuity in English/British government but with it the suffocating weight of the empiricism of the ages; it also points to how recently our public institutions were clawed free of the aristocratic embrace and post-1688 monarchy's extraordinary historical success in conflating dynastic-private and public purpose.

Not a taxman by background, Montagu was a transitional figure in the Inland Revenue. Under him it had struggled to shed old ways of treating the public. Once the taxpayer was objectified, treated as potentially dishonest. Now the watchword is 'customer', an even more peculiarly inapt metaphor in this context of non-choice. But lately this key department of state has become a giver. It is now a social policy department dispensing benefits (tax credits) and policing the minimum wage.

This work, exacting money and dispensing income, is the very nub of state, the engine room of social democracy. But of course you can hold a lengthy conversation with this high official without that word 'state' being used, without his needing to speak of a wider public entity or wrap his department into a structure of authority, into a synoptic history of government. So the state is tacit; this is just an English civil servant practising public administration, embarrassed at abstraction (yet Montagu was an academic philosopher to the age of 30).

No, there is something dysfunctional here, in this non-reference, in this language gap. How can Montagu conceive departmental purpose, derive a strategy, adduce the reason for the Revenue, without reference to state? What

© The Political Quarterly Publishing Co. Ltd. 2004

Published by Blackwell Publishing Ltd, 9600 Garsington Road, Oxford OX4 2DQ, UK and 350 Main Street, Malden, MA 02148, USA

can his presence at those regular Wednesday meetings of permanent secretaries mean if he and they are not, in some measure, conducting the business of state? Specifically, he remains the butt and creature of the hierarchs in the Treasury unless he and they understand themselves in a wider scheme of state.

Citizens lose from this omission, too. Fiscal comprehension is reduced—and, surely, in understanding tax tolerance grows. As the gatherer of tax the Inland Revenue has a responsibility to persuade, inform, even warm the public to its purposes, which of course are not its, but the state's. A few years back, I had discussed with Montagu a proposal to issue along with income-tax forms an abbreviated guide to where the spending goes. A pie chart might elucidate the thing and, perhaps, enlighten the public about their government. It has not happened. A precondition of its happening is state—an intellectual and administrative awakening to the concept.

Another glance. On a street near the *Guardian* a man in shirtsleeves rushes out of an office doorway towards a parked car. A mundane urban playlet unfolds. Moments later, he hares past me towards the ambling figure of an Islington borough council traffic warden who has just, evidently, ticketed his vehicle. The man grabs the warden by the arm. I pass and say 'don't push him' and—I claim no causality—what might have been an assault becomes a sheepish remonstrance by the motorist. This, too, is a vignette of our state. That warden carried the authority of public office, executing a task enjoined by collective will for the common good. In performing it, he was buffeted and despised. One reason is that he was the state unnamed, unexpressed, a thing of fragments of power and dissipated authority. Nothing connected the warden's green-trimmed Islington cap with larger purpose. He was not labelled or fortified. Islington: what do aggressive motorists care about borough boundaries? The missing link is the state, not just as an idea but—a commercial analogy, because we live in a commercial society—a brand. We lack a state identity that carries over from encounter to encounter with public offices, common signage that makes connections along the frontier between the private and the public, the individual and the collective.

How often does Islington council tell itself or the people who live in the borough (let alone those who use its streets) that it is part of the wider public 'thing'? Would that thought even be intelligible to the (Liberal Democrat) leader of the council; it would certainly be hateful. The chief executive of Islington belongs to Solace, the Society of Local Authority Chief Executives, but that professional association, the repository of local statehood, exists in splendid isolation, joined occasionally and randomly with groups of other state servants, struggling to identify itself. She and it are weaker, less able to accomplish their local purposes, as a result.

In any conceivable scheme for governing a country as big and complex as the UK there are bound to be sites and opportunities for conflict and confusion between the different parts of government. Elected or appointed, local service managers will always have grounds for complaint about the centre and vice versa. Statehood cannot trump geography or functional specialisation. But some common sense of statehood would lubricate the gears. And the public might understand more. 'State' might tear that thick veil of ignorance about the division of labour between public entities. Public understanding—public willingness to be taxed—would be much greater if, occasionally, Islington wore the garb (even a lapel badge) of a single, bigger entity.

What these examples say is that our daily connection with the state is broken-backed. It wears no single piece of identification and we do not have a clue what is what. The traffic warden and the taxman inhabit the same public space; the employment of one may depend on the efforts of the other, but would they recognise each other (to form a common cause, to project their purposes to the public) or be recognised for the jobs they do? To say they are all in the public sector or inhabit the public space is not good enough.

Examples abound of how the absence of a state concept and a parallel administrative form confound and diminish our capacity for concerted action in the public space, let alone progressive politics. Key institutions of state brandish their particularity, their distance from each other, sometimes even that they by their own lights are not part of the public space. They do it in colour: those salmon-coloured coats worn by doormen at the Bank of England in Threadneedle Street (last time I visited they were all male) shout non-belonging. What has been, since 1946, a 'nationalised industry' is not, it would appear, part of the state. Yes, there is an issue here about its title. Why is the United Kingdom's central bank so misnamed? The asymmetries of England, Scotland, Northern Ireland, Wales and the UK are part of but not the whole explanation for absence of state.

Is it a Cheshire cat? The animal may own the Crown Estate, the paths among the trees on Forestry Commission tracts and the hectares of grass and tarmac behind the signs specifying a place 'within the meaning of the Official Secrets Act'? But what sort of creature encompasses at one and the same time the British Broadcasting Corporation and the Health Development Agency but not the Financial Services Authority (which is classed as private sector) or London Metropolitan University? Taxonomy may be a blood sport; bound-aries matter, and not just for tax and borrowing. But too much can be made of the fuzziness of the state's outer edges. Even though it may be hard to see where the beast's shaggy coat touches the ground, everyone can still see it is a saluki.

Argument

In this short contribution, the line of argument is as follows. If 'it is no longer clear what the public and public service mean in British politics',[1] statehood (as idea and constitutional reassembly) is a remedy. It is because we lack the apparatus and appurtenances of 'state' that public purposes are harder to realise in Britain. Absence of state is an element in policy failure. A stronger idea of state is a precondition for success, in public health, migration management, housing (land allocation), redistributions of income and opportunity, market regulation, security.

Here is a diagnosis of our missing state:

- Jurisdictions comparable to the UK have to contend with the division of administrative labour between centre and locality/region, coherence among public agencies, and the boundaries of the public sphere. Some comparable countries are monarchies; in others it is hard to say that traditions of 'citizenship' are stronger than in the UK. The case for UK constitutional exceptionalism cannot be assumed. Yet there are distinctly English/British absences and deformations in thinking and acting statehood. What the state's staff can tell themselves about what they are doing, let alone tell the public they serve, tax and regulate, is truncated.
- The centre left bears specific responsibility for confusion, even antagonism to the idea and practice of statehood, which is all the more remarkable since for much of the twentieth century it claimed the state as its own. This had partly to do with lack of joined-up thinking on the part of the democratic left about power and governance together with dogmatism further left, drawing on Marxian refusal to contemplate really existing states, and with liberal ambiguity about the exercise of public powers for ordering and controlling, which has often veered into mindless liberty-ism or, lately, a devotion to individual rights to be exercised against the state.
- British public life has been characterised by practical make-do and mend, muddling through—administrative empiricism coupled with an inverted arrogance on the part of public officials in refusing to think through their identities, mutual relationship. Departmentalism and the unjoined-up nature of service provision stem from weakness in the generic identity of public sector staff. Part of this story is administrative particularism expressed in conflicts between central and local government, which is in part a tale of class.

The rest of this essay consists of suggestions for the (re)construction of statehood based on (1) some common or garden observations about signage or 'branding' and state phenomenology; (2) the need to move forward now that the nostrums of the new public management are being discarded; and (3) the dawning realisation among public officials of common interests and the need for common formation—in order to dissolve 'joining up' problems.

Why we are stateless

State history

This is well-trodden ground. As if exhausted by the upheavals of the mid-seventeenth century—or stupefied by the clarity of the Revolution—political actors in England and Scotland slumbered under the wispy vapours of 'Crown in Parliament', prerogative powers and the like. Chartism guttered and set no flares alight among the middle classes. The rise of Labour did not bring the replacement of subjection by citizenship. Neither liberalism nor Labourism challenged aristocratic-hieratic models of administrative behaviour, which stunted the growth of a common culture of state service.

If in the sixteenth century the increasing numbers of professionals employed in government provided impersonal, pervasive and accreting activity on behalf of government rather than of a particular ruler,[2] this did not give rise—except perhaps during a few decades in the seventeenth century—to an English or British state idea. An anonymous paper of 1621 noted 'This word "State" was larned by our neighbourhood and commerce with the Low Countreys, as if we were, or affected to be governed by States. This the Queen saw and hated.' Her successors and their servants ditto.

Thus the great crises of what became the British state such as 1745–6, the two decades from 1795, and 1911–14 were in a profound sense unspoken. War may have helped cause the growth of government but not of governmental consciousness. Is that to say any more than that the dynasty succeeded and the social agreements underpinning British nineteenth century government forms (which we still have) were profound; therefore they did not need to speak? Within England the expansion of central government stimulated and in turn was stimulated by local self-government. This coexistence was (and remains) founded on a mass of fiscal, political and administrative paradoxes, but none of them was ever enough to provoke deep thought about statehood. Similarly, the mystery of England, Britain and the United Kingdom; if it hangs together why ask questions?

Twentieth century Britain 'worked'. Prime ministers, judges and constitutional commentators, unchallenged, saw no need to define or explicate the architecture of public power and, when they wrote learned tomes, felt it sufficient to base their arguments on misty and tautological 'convention'. What was it that taxed and borrowed, issued coinage and credit, prosecuted and imprisoned and, as if it were immortal, promised to pay pensions a generation hence, yet (they had to believe) could be steered and reshaped by contingently elected and short-stay politicians? John Dunn scolds those after 'some would-be integrative theoretical conception of the state';[3] but what if all we have in Britain are variants on Peter Hennessy's apothegm that the constitution is procedure or tautology along the lines that the state is what politicians and officials and judges do? But now if British empiricism has not reached the end of the road, it must be in the final straight. Conventions no longer hold. Professors of procedure have long vacated their chairs. Doing anything much depends on a better, and a better articulated, idea of state.

The state and the left

Our state is impoverished thanks, in measure, to the left. Marxists (here) either dismissed it as a 'committee of the bourgeoisie' or (there) turned the proverbial blind eye to totalitarian state form and practice. Socialists venerated state ownership but turned out not to have thought much about it, which helps explain the practical failures of nationalisation and what turned out to be for the half century after 1945 Labour's deep constitutional conservatism. Social democrats have tended to confusion, at one and the same time disdaining statehood in the shape of police and prison officers, while hoping to spend the proceeds of its tax and customs officers. Fear of oppression by the only thing capable of ameliorating the life chances of the disadvantaged was—and remains—uncomfortable.

Labour used to fear that the state had been infected by aristocracy or conservatism (approximately the Bennite position) but devoted very little thought to how to organise public services, as was shown by the 1980s episode when the 'new left' acquired municipal power. It is extraordinary that, for all the contumely heaped on Fabian centralism, it has been little developed in Labour thinking or Labour government practice. The same applies to whatever its converse might be. Where, for example, were teachers placed in the Labour state tradition? The party resisted the proposal that teachers deliver a national (state) curriculum; recent debate about the financing of higher education has mostly refused to address the tender question of whether universities are part of the state. Behind both examples lies squeamishness about public power but also enervating uncertainty about what social democracy is about.

If state power is inherently oppressive and needs to be corralled, constrained or undercut by various pluralisms, what space does this leave for progressive policies which rely, no two ways about it, on the exaction of money from possessors? Taxation as Labour understood it was an expression of obligation to community (through the state) as well as the means for a democracy to achieve agreement about a fair distribution of rewards in a market economy. 'To pursue these ends in a society whose political culture has been shaped by individualism rather than collectivism and where private property has complex and deep foundations was to explore the limits of political action.'[4] Taxation is what states do. But Labour, old and new, has never accepted the syllogism that if the results of taxation (public goods and services) are worth celebrating, then so is the entity which alone can take and give.

For the likes of David Marquand civil society is the realm of freedom, while the state is an agent of oppression.[5] But what if civil society (encompassing markets) is also the realm of injustice? Marquand shudders: the state may be necessary, for regulating markets for example, but its capacity for diminishing blessed liberty will soon show. A recent expression of this way of thinking has been (often directed against Home Secretary David Blunkett) a stout defence of liberty menaced by the state's police officers, magistrates and jailers. Social democrats seem sometimes to think that the secret policemen and the social workers are not employed by the same entity, divvying up the same revenue stream; but both, if their purposes are sound, deserve respect as agents of state.

Administrative empiricism

The state has not been well served, conceptually at any rate, by its own employees. In cartoon form, let me pick out some strands from administrative history and practice. One is masochism. Government officials have too easily worn the clothes of put-upon 'ours not to reason why' functionaries. The collective silence of civil servants (there are parallels among council officials) at moments of redefinition, such as the enunciation of the Armstrong doctrine in 1986, did statehood no favours. Eunuchs may be functional in absolutist Ottoman conditions but not where the state has a cultural battle on its hands and needs to project a sense of the excitement of public service.

Another is class. Whitehall has exemplified social division, the separation of state officials into sheep and goats, and prized attitude and demeanour above function and effect. (The Northcote–Trevelyan reforms of 1850–70 were as much about conserving a social bias in the state's service as modernisation.) The cult of the gentleman and weakness of the forces of administrative reform at moments of crisis (1916–19, 1939–42) left no rational basis for the civil service as such. No one, the Treasury included, can give reasons for ending its ranks at one place which is the reason why 'civil service numbers' has become an oxymoronic plaything for politicians seeking a cheap hit, in or out of office. Moving staff from headquarters, where they are civil servants, to external agencies, where they are not, despite doing the same work, has become a sport. But a result of this has been fragmentation of administrative culture and loss of confidence. State officials have, on occasion, to exhibit elite behaviour: to know more (for why else would the state plan, educate, change public behaviour). The elitism Whitehall once carried off is no longer possible; its conventions have worn away. A precondition of some refashioning of the public service identity is an idea of the state. And that will have large consequences for the local state; it might even shock the personnel of local authorities into accepting that is what they indeed are. They might see that a cause of the suspicion and lack of regard in which local government is held is not 'centralisation' but the pretence that councils are not organs of state, with the same goals, styles and fiscal dynamics as a host of other public bodies.

A third deformation in the vitals of the British state is excessive audit and inspection. The success of inspectorial models in securing improvements to public health in the mid-nineteenth century helps explain the embedding of a culture of double-counting and quantitative explication. It has in turns fed and been fed by England's strongly anti-collective popular or rather 'Rother-mere' culture: if the auditors point a finger, newspapers have been happy to join in blaming. A financial regulator such as the National Audit Office, answering to the House of Commons' Public Accounts Committee, tends to accentuate the negative, harping on failure, elevating neo-platonic ideals of efficiency. The NAO operates as if it were not also an organ of state, part of a common endeavour—with shared responsibility for state purposes.

What is to be done?

To the Tory assault on quangos in the early Thatcher period was added, in the 1990s, a left-liberal critique of unaccountable, appointed government 'by moonlight'.[6] It needs reviving, less for the sake of greater accountability than for the sake of greater coherence in the projection and presentation of government to people. It's not just proliferation of public bodies but com-petition among them, division of purposes, fragmentation of services. Who comprehends the connection between Connexions, Sure Start and the Chil-dren's Fund, which are meant, together, to improve life chances for deprived children and young people from birth to 18? This is more than a matter of New Labour politicians having the lungs for blowing a trumpet—fearing fiscal retribution if they are too noisy about what they are up to. The artifice of government reduces understanding.

A population of bodies has been created that increase costs (because of duplication and competition) and confuse the public. There is no defensible division of labour, say, between the Audit Commission and the Commission on Healthcare Audit and Inspection; those regulated are overburdened and the public are nonplussed. Do either belong to a common public endeavour? They exist as they do partly because of the growth during the past two decades of the cult—it does have some elements of religious faith—of 'independence'. Within the state, so the argument runs, need to be created islands from which non-state personalities albeit working with state resources should adjudge state functions. In the British way of things, the obvious question—On what basis are these independent judgements made and to whom are the independents accountable?—remains unposed.

The argument is a simple one. If staff had a stronger connection with state, they would be more likely to cooperate. If they understood their work as entelechy, the practical and functional realisation of the bigger project of state . . . Sophisticated and effective programmes will require complex adminis-tration. State is not a panacea against complexity. It certainly would not make delivery any easier. For the state to intervene successfully in the lives of low income pre-school children such that their chances of succeeding at school approach those of their middle income contemporaries is and will always be a massive challenge. But the success and certainly the sustainability of the programme attempting to meet it, Sure Start, depend on its being recognised and appreciated a long way from the deprived wards in which it operates. Winning recognition would be easier if (in Sure Start's title or administration?) some link were made to the state's unique interest in the wellbeing of children, which has to do with its own identity in time as the guarantor of intergenerational equity.

Statehood has a public face and an inner identity. The latter, first. Public service is broken into shards: the civil service, health care, local government, public bodies at large, all with their own patterns of recruitment, formation and culture. Take the Society of Local Authority Chief Executives. Its members are key agents of the state. Through them public services are delivered and key processes (parliamentary elections, for example) are run. But are public servants collegial? They are close kin to other managers and officials, but the relationship goes unacknowledged, the common genes unexpressed. Their capacity and self-confidence suffer; the state is diminished.

The case in principle for a common identity for state officials rests on economy. The overall costs of managing the state would be less if there were greater interchangeability of staff between different bodies. Talent would be maximised if boundaries to movement, between Whitehall, local government, the NHS, were lowered. The case rests on effectiveness, too. Public officials with a stronger sense of belonging to a wider enterprise would likely be more secure and more likely to accept innovations in ways of working or institutional change. In all his barnstorming about reform, Tony Blair never seems to have cottoned on to this: security of identity makes for greater receptiveness to messages about change.

This points to common training, either at the point of induction or in-service, or, at the very least, to a growth in the number of occasions when managers and administrators from different branches of government come together to, implicitly, recognise a common identity. Some recent small steps have been taken by the Cabinet Office to encourage dialogue between those responsible for management training in health, the civil service, the police and defence. Vastly more could be done. But among the preconditions is the Cabinet Office's acceptance of a role as the impresario of state and that in turn depends on the remnants of civil service hierarchy (contempt for lesser beings in the administrative food chain) being finally overturned. For that to happen, progressive politicians would have to see that the state—a new articulation of statehood—is a hinge for realising their own purposes. New Labour has treated interest in state form as somehow effete, airy-fairy business for which those concerned with implementing delivery have no time. Perhaps as they realise how difficult 'delivery' is, they will also see this connection.

Service delivery will always be based on specialisms and bounded, sometimes esoteric, knowledge. Teachers will always be formed differently from fire officers; auditors will be accredited some cultural distance from nurses. But functional specialisation need not exclude common identification. State service is, as it were, supra-professional. Perhaps there will always be a tense boundary, within the state, between professionalism—the claim for autonomy of action which professions make—and central authority. But some thinking about the balance of interests would be a start. It is no longer enough to rely on convention, the assumption that say police officers consider themselves part of a wider public space. A thorough review of training would show up the tendency towards autarky, hence the need, in induction training and thereafter, to remind the state's staff of the nature of their ultimate employer.

The British are supposed to be squeamish about uniforms. Senior officials of HM Customs and Excise have them, and swords, but keep them hidden away in a bottom drawer for rare fancy dress occasions. Perhaps there is not much scope for common visual identifiers for state officials—badges. But it might be worthwhile (especially for those on the centre left) to pause for a moment and ask why they would find risible or threatening the idea that state staff had a single brooch or lapel badge. Why not common signage? A walker in the English woods might see a sign for Forest Enterprise, formerly the agency of Forestry Commission, which in turn is a department of the Department for Environment, Food and Rural Affairs. What do those entities contribute to understanding the provision of public benefit through state ownership and communal payment? Would it be outlandish to stamp the Forestry Commission noticeboard with a super-sign indicating state enterprise. On notice boards across the countries: 'this road/forest/hospital . . . is brought to you by the British state'. The European Commission does as much. How much do we exaggerate public comprehension and fail to realise the value of repeated, binary images?

Conclusion

Recovery of self-confidence about the public realm is indispensable for any serious politics, whether right or left, Andrew Gamble concludes. But it's not that vague 'realm', with all its monarchical Shakespearian associations, that needs recovery; it is state. And is 'recovery' the right word? Was there ever a time when the state was celebrated?

In his book *Decline of the Public* David Marquand gives up the ghost, trying to conjure instead some cosy local, mutual coming together. He even gives up on progressive taxation. History, he argues, in what sounds like a counsel of despair, might inspire some more radical way of changing civil society than a return to the time-warped Fabian notion of redistributive taxation, a good enough cause in the days of Lloyd George, but hardly one which is going to bring the millions out on to the streets today. But who then is going to pay for the public goods he still craves, the transport, public libraries? If the answer is municipalities, try telling that to the poor districts without a viable base for charges or taxation (even assuming there is popular will for this).

The central state is not going to wither away. What we have already seen of the first decades of the twenty-first century confirm that. It is not just security in the face of imported threat of a kind that only an organised, coherent, policed state can provide. When it comes to movement of people, goods and capital, there is nothing else around. Health and higher education, quintessential public goods, require both uniformities and their contrary, that is to say discriminations in funding between recipients of a kind that only central authority can accomplish. The state needs to be built up, not demolished. This is not a matter of ideological sero-conversion among progressive politicians, though some affirmation of the benefits if not the glory of collective endeavour would help. There is much that the state's staff could do, for themselves and the wider world. Confidence is their means and their prize. Pride in working for the government and an end to back-foot defensiveness can be engendered. But before the re-validation of public service can begin, before much-needed intellectual effort is put into framing and fashioning the new century's public space, we need a concept of state.

Notes

1 A. Gamble, *Between Europe and America*, London, Palgrave Macmillan, 2003, p. 231.
2 J. H. Elliott, *Europe Divided 1559–1598*, London, Collins, 1968, p. 81.
3 J. Dunn, *The Cunning of Unreason*, London, HarperCollins, 2000, p. 109.
4 R. Whiting, *The Labour Party and Taxation*, Cambridge, Cambridge University Press, 2000, p. 273.
5 D. Marquand, *Decline of the Public: The Hollowing Out of Citizenship*, Cambridge, Polity Press, 2004.
6 P. Birkinshaw, I. Harden and N. Lewis, *Government by Moonlight*, London, Unwin Hyman, 1990.

The State and the Market

JOHN KAY

What should be the boundaries between the state and the market? To pose this question is to dictate the form of the answer, because it requires that it is both possible and desirable to define distinct public and private spheres of activity. The immediate implication is that the interactions between them can be managed through regulation and contract.

This philosophy has led in the last two decades to a reformulation of the political agenda. Traditional boundaries between public and private activities have been reassessed: the assumption is that through regulation and contract it may be possible to carve out large areas of traditional public sector activity for private businesses. Since private businesses are assumed generally to be more efficient and innovative—and there is a good deal of evidence to support that assertion—the framework points to privatisation as a central direction of public service reform.

In this chapter, I argue that it is a mistake to seek such well defined boundaries. The question assumes that there is a fundamental dichotomy between public and private sector organisations, that such bodies are and should be managed in different ways, and that they are populated by different kinds of people who display different kinds of behaviour. While there is much truth in that observation, there should not be. The better route to public service reform is one which restores elements of public service ethos to parts of the private sector, and establishes greater scope for innovation and for pluralism in the public sector.

The areas in which it has seemed necessary to define or redefine private and public roles fall into several categories. There are conventional areas of public service provision—such as health and education. Utilities such as transport and electricity have sometimes been managed by public sector bodies but are now more frequently undertaken by private companies. And activities such as pharmaceuticals and professional services are usually undertaken by private companies, but such wide and general questions of public policy arise that the activities of firms are extensively regulated, and the management of such regulation is central to the management of these activities.

But in all of these areas, the best performing organisations have generally been hybrid bodies, which combine elements of public service ethos with private sector innovation and enterprise. To list Stanford University, Bell Laboratories, Massachusetts General Hospital, Compagnie General des Eaux, Swiss Railways, Merck, Johnson and Johnson, British building societies, German regional banks, J. P. Morgan and Fannie Mae, is to give only a preliminary sense of the scope and variety of such hybrids. But the list is sufficiently long, and the achievements of the organisations on it sufficiently

© The Political Quarterly Publishing Co. Ltd. 2004

74   Published by Blackwell Publishing Ltd, 9600 Garsington Road, Oxford OX4 2DQ, UK and 350 Main Street, Malden, MA 02148, USA

impressive, to suggest that the demand for clarity in relations between public and private sector is not self-evidently justified.

The purposes of government

The desire to find such a sharp demarcation between public and private activities stems from a belief that the nature of public and private institutions is fundamentally distinct. Business people are risk takers, entrepreneurial but greedy; bureaucrats are risk averse, unimaginative but concerned for the public good. More extreme versions of this position do not concede even a public service motivation to public servants: government employees occupy their posts only because they lack the ability or energy to perform successfully in the private sector.

The differentiation in the nature of institutions follows naturally from the conventional differentiation of activities. The traditional functions of the state were to wage war, adjudicate disputes, and levy taxes to finance these functions. And government still does these things: but they are not now the principal things it does. Today we look to government to secure the provision of education and a transport infrastructure, to guarantee us medical treatment and security in old age, to organise the collection of rubbish and assure unfailing supplies of electricity. The main role of government today is in the provision of goods and services, rather than the exercise of authority.

This transition has extensive ramifications. In the exercise of authority, the legitimacy of that authority and the propriety of the process by which it is exercised are fundamental. We want judges and policemen to follow the law, we want soldiers to obey orders, we want tax inspectors to implement the tax code. But in the delivery of services, our primary concern is with outcome, not process. We want to send our children to good schools; we want the bus to come on time, the rubbish to go and the lights to stay on. We want to face retirement with confidence, and to get better when we are ill.

The mechanisms through which these results are achieved are secondary. Most people are not very interested in how their hospital is run, just as they are not very interested in how their supermarket is run. Their concern in both cases is that the organisation concerned, hospital or supermarket, delivers the goods and services they want.

Systems of public management have largely failed to respond to this change in the nature of state functions. The process oriented mechanisms needed for the proper exercise of legitimate authority are ill suited to the effective delivery of goods and services. Judges could reach conclusions much more quickly and tax inspectors could collect revenue much more cheaply if less attention was paid to the propriety of the process, but we do not want them to do this: we are concerned with how the result is achieved as much as with the result itself. But efficiency and effectiveness are the criteria we properly apply to the delivery of services.

The legitimacy of economic power

This transition in the nature of government function poses problems for both right and left. The right is suspicious of the state as provider of services, and wishes to limit that role. Nervous of the role of government, it seeks to limit its extent by emphasising the traditional process concerns of the public administrator. The resulting inefficiency is almost a virtue, because it constrains the effectiveness of the state. The left encounters a different problem, a legacy of the history of Marxist socialism. This is the issue of the legitimacy of the private exercise of economic power.

Actions are legitimate if there is a good and widely accepted answer to the question 'What gives them the right to do that?' For a century, the legitimacy of corporate and management authority was a central political question. The purpose of organised labour, of trades unions and political parties, was to challenge the basis on which private entrepreneurs exercised seemingly arbitrary authority over individuals and used their political power to reinforce that authority. The class struggle defined the roles of political parties and the nature of political rhetoric.

These arguments no longer have much resonance in rich Western economies and if the legitimacy of corporate and management authority is an issue today, it is an issue of a quite different kind: an issue of relationships between managers and other stakeholders rather than between labour and capital. The old arguments have died because of fundamental changes in society and economy. Geographic mobility is greatly increased; patterns of consumption, work and credit are more flexible; the assets of a business are embedded in its people rather than its machinery. In consequence, competitive markets perform many of the functions which once seemed to require political action. If you don't like a job, or its pay, or its conditions of employment, you find another one. If the milkman waters the milk, the brewer salts the beer, you can take your custom elsewhere. And competition is today the principal mechanism through which private economic power is controlled. The organisation of labour and legislation to regulate economic activity helped to improve working conditions, secure product quality and fair prices; but so did competitive markets. And, to the chagrin and eventual defeat of socialists, the market economy proved more effective than centralised political control in achieving their aims—a favourable working environment, the goods and services consumers want. And that is why it is the delivery of goods and services by the public sector, not the private sector, which is at the centre of political debate today. Customers of private sector goods and services take for granted a process of continuous improvement and of responsiveness to changing requirements. They cannot make similar assumptions about public sector provision.

Business has won legitimacy through success. We accept, even welcome, the authority of Sainsbury and Tesco in delivering our groceries because of the manifest effectiveness with which they have done this in the past. In ensuring food safety, consumers now have more trust in supermarkets, which are competing to sustain their reputation, than they have in government. We do not challenge what they do because, in the main, we like what they do and have alternatives if we do not. In a modern service economy, legitimacy may be earned by meeting our needs as consumers. What is legitimate is what works, and this is true in both public and private sectors.

Motives and functions

There is some truth in the stereotypes of the dynamic but self-interested business person and the public spirited but ineffective public servant. But if both business and government are primarily concerned with the delivery of services to the public, this distinction makes no sense. Our objective should be to change these caricatures rather than to build institutions around them.

Services of all kinds—health or hamburgers, education or electricity—are best delivered by people who care about the quality of the service they provide. In the private sector, purely instrumental motivation is rarely successful in the long run. This is an easy lesson to forget. The development and decline of mass production assembly lines demonstrated two decades ago how highly incentivised but boring work led to endless labour disputes and a workforce with no commitment to the final product. In more recent times, complex bonus schemes for managers not only led to fraud and rapacity but—as in those car plants—created destructive tensions within organisations. Great businesses are built and sustained only by people who are committed to the business, its products and its customers; and such people are needed both on the shop floor and in the board room.

The instrumental view of the purposes of the corporation led to the destruction of once great businesses like ICI and GEC, and to the well recorded frauds at Enron and WorldCom. The same philosophy brought about an environment in which banks and insurance companies have lost the confidence of their customers and the loyalty of their employees, and pharmaceutical businesses look at pipelines largely empty of important innovations. These changes followed inescapably as the perception that financial service companies and drug manufacturers existed in the first instance to serve the public gave way to the view that their primary purpose was the creation of shareholder value.

Similar issues emerged in the privatisation of state monopolies. The authority of such bodies is derived neither from democratic election nor success in a competitive marketplace. In consequence, they have mostly failed to establish the legitimacy they automatically enjoyed as public agencies. Such absence of popular support or confidence, which led the public to turn on Railtrack whenever anything went wrong on Britain's railways, was the fundamental cause of the failure of rail privatisation in the UK.

Most people—in the public or private sector—value material reward. They also value the respect of colleagues and customers, and the satisfaction of a job well done. And successful organisations—public or private—are those which effectively meet this variety of needs of both users and providers. In some public services—like health and education—it is particularly important to us that the service is delivered by someone who cares. These services will be most effectively provided if we take advantage of that ethos of public service.

But public service here means service to the public, rather than the provision of services by the public sector. And traditionally such an ethos of service to the public was found in professional service activities such as law, accountancy or education; in health care, whether provided by private companies or public agencies; in the management and operation of utilities and infrastructure, again whether provided by public companies or private agencies. But where such services were provided by profit-making agencies, the ethos of professionalism has recently come under pressure from the commercialisation which follows from an instrumental view of the purposes of private business.

On the one hand, we see growing emphasis on the instrumental provision of service by individuals motivated by financial incentives. On the other, we yearn for an expression of genuine concern for the quality of the product, the interests of customers, and the integrity of the organisation which delivers the product and meets the needs of those customers. The difference is one we notice. We learn to discount the synthetic 'have a nice day' of the fast food outlet and distinguish the smiling life insurance salesman from the trusted financial adviser. And that is why so many instrumental corporations have failed, even in their own terms.

Our purpose should therefore be to elide rather than emphasise differences between public and private sector organisations. In Britain and in some other countries there has been an almost obsessive attempt to shoehorn every possible activity into a corporate framework and to assume that all functions must be clearly labelled public or private. In consequence, these artificial structures were imposed on businesses where neither the capital structure nor the governance structure of a plc is appropriate and the reforms in question have subsequently failed—as in water, the railways, nuclear power and air traffic control. There is now a pressing requirement for new, more flexible organisational structures in health, education and other traditional public services, which offer more management autonomy and financial freedom. This has led in Britain to the reinvention, in a disjointed manner, of a variety of hybrid structures. We need, not two forms of organisation—the government agency and the plc—but a spectrum adapted to the different kinds of services which are delivered and the different market environments and funding structures within which they operate.

The objective should be to substitute across that whole spectrum of hybrid activity an ethos of service to the public as customers: an ethos which should replace both the instrumental motivations which are justifiably mistrusted in the private sector, and the emphasis on process over outcome still too often encountered in the public sector. Public sector reform has led to a recognition that users, not politicians, are the people to whom those who deliver services are properly accountable—symbolised, not insignificantly, in the redesignation of rail passengers and telephone subscribers as customers. This focus on customers is a major achievement of the more successful privatisations, although privatisation is neither necessary nor sufficient for this result. Public sector reform has brought greater recognition that taxpayers should be treated as consumers in some functions—even tax collection—where privatisation is inappropriate and competition impossible.

The sources of innovation[1]

We do not want our tax inspectors, judges and soldiers to be imaginative and innovative: we want them to conform to rules and structures that have been centrally established. But we do want these characteristics of imagination and innovation in our teachers and our doctors, and in the people who create and manage our transport infrastructure. The principal reason the private sector has a better record of innovation than the public is not the different objectives of private and public organisations, nor the different kinds of people who work in them; it is the result of differences in the way these organisations are structured.

Centrally planned economies fell hopelessly behind market economies in consumer oriented innovation. Planning seeks to assimilate alternative views of the future into a coherent narrative: to 'speak with a single voice'.[2] Markets proceed through disciplined pluralism, which permits uncontrolled experiment but rapidly terminates such experiments when they fail. And they generally do fail: most innovations do not work, technically or commercially. Large organisations, public or private, quite legitimately find good reasons not to embark on them. When they do, for motives which generally have a veneer of high rationality but in fact more often reflect a changing balance of political forces, public sector innovations are frequently undertaken on an inappropriately large scale.

Under centralised management feedback is poor, because decision makers and those who report to them do not wish to hear, or pass on, bad news. The outcome is the conflation of conflicting opinions into the single voice and the suppression of honest reporting. Such characteristics were common to the human disaster of Mao's Great Leap Forward and the commercial disaster of Britain's nuclear power generation programme and are replicated, with less extreme consequences, throughout public sector organisations and large private businesses.

If China's Great Leap Forward caricatures the failures of planning, the evolution of the personal computer industry exemplifies the successes of the market. Its central feature was a haphazard process of development which no one controlled, and in which almost all predictions of future developments were quickly falsified. Most innovations were commercially unsuccessful for those who devised them—even those which ultimately proved key to the emergence of the industry we see today, such as the invention of the general purpose microprocessor, the graphical user interface, and the promotion of a universal operating standard.

The process of disciplined pluralism, which allows continuous waves of incremental experiment and rapid feedback on the performance of that experiment, explains why modern market economies offer such a wide range of consumer goods. The absence of such a process explains why, despite the Soviet Union's capabilities in defence oriented science, no remotely comparable developments occurred there. The difference in innovative capacity is not the result of a difference in motivation—in practice, financial incentives seem to have played a rather minor role in major twentieth century innovations (and the financial rewards from such major innovations were mostly modest). The largest rewards from innovation went to companies (such as Microsoft and Glaxo) that successfully marketed innovation rather than to the innovators themselves. The real issue is the contrast between planning and centralisation on the one hand, and pluralism and decentralisation on the other. The key dynamic of the market economy, and the primary source of its success, is the power of disciplined pluralism.

Disciplined pluralism

We sometimes talk of the 'marketplace in ideas'. The metaphor identifies the most important characteristic of a marketplace: not the jingle of cash registers, but the effect of disciplined pluralism in promoting innovation and in discriminating between success and failures. In the marketplace for ideas new concepts are constantly floated, most of them wrong or foolish, all subject to assessment and evaluation. A few survive these tests, and knowledge advances.

The modern marketplace for ideas came into being when the disciplined pluralism of scientific rationalism replaced the single voice of religious authority. The development of disciplined pluralism in intellectual life was contemporaneous with commercial innovation in applied science and in the development of business organisations, and this is not a coincidence. The coevolution of technology with economic, social and political institutions has been the essential dynamic of Western societies since the Renaissance and Reformation.

Democracy itself is a marketplace in political leadership. Representative democracy acknowledges the need for political leadership and authority, but insists that the ideas which leaders implement and the authority they exercise are regularly contested. Ideological diversity and personal ambition provide pluralism; the electoral process provides discipline.

And disciplined pluralism applies not just within the institutions of the market economy, but to the development of the institutions of liberal capitalism themselves. The convergence of almost all developed societies on a democratic model which gives governments renewable tenure in office of four to five years illustrates how the shape of institutions is itself determined by processes of experiment, choice and selection in a pluralist environment.

The competitive market for goods and services is the most familiar example of disciplined pluralism. By distributing economic authority to many agents in competitive markets, it allows free experiment in the manufacture and distribution of products and in the organisation of their production. The discipline of this pluralism comes from the interaction of the market for goods and services with the market for capital, which terminates unsuccessful ventures by depriving them of finance.

The evolution of health care demonstrates two different models of disciplined pluralism. Pharmacology proceeds by the competitive development of innovations by private corporations. The process is highly regulated and protected by patents and commercial secrecy. Patent legislation creates competitive pluralism characterised by artificially created but lively competition, discipline is provided by regulatory authorities and clinical choice. Though far from ideal, this is a model of disciplined pluralism which has proved successful in practice; by comparison, centrally planned economies performed very poorly in pharmaceutical innovation.

Surgery and treatment protocols advance through piecemeal innovation by individual practitioners and teams, with almost no formal regulation, and open sharing of methods and results in a peer review process. Both styles of innovative mechanism work: the central problem of the management of health care everywhere is that organisational innovation has failed to keep pace with technological innovation.

The interaction of the intellectual pluralism of modern scientific thought, the political pluralism of democracy, and the economic pluralism of competitive markets, has produced the coevolution of institutions which is the basis of technological advance and economic growth. Anonymity is a common feature of all these mechanisms of pluralism. In the marketplace for ideas, the outcome is the verdict of many appraisers; in the marketplace for political leadership, the outcome is the verdict of many voters; in the marketplace for goods and services, the outcome is the verdict of many consumers.

The anonymity of disciplined pluralism is infuriating to people who rail against the impersonality of market forces. And it is constantly challenged by those who seek to replace competitive markets by monopolies—those in government who feel the need of the single voice that can control outcomes and respond to central direction, those individuals who would wish to be that single voice. Authoritarian figures on both left and right repeatedly try to dictate the course of scholarship, dominate political leadership, and control the evolution of their industries. And, for a time, some of them succeed. The price of progress is constant vigilance in support of free enquiry, democratic election, and genuinely competitive marketplaces.

There are many other examples of disciplined pluralism. Universities compete with each other to establish reputations. The pluralism of US higher education has substantially outperformed the centralisation of Europe. The discipline of its pluralism is provided by a competitive marketplace for the brightest students and the most capable faculty. This is but one example—from the not-for-profit sector—of how the disciplined pluralism involved in the creation of brands and reputations fosters innovation and raises standards. Doctors and museums, sports clubs and cities, compete with each other in similar ways.

Disciplined pluralism is an evolutionary process. The extraordinary intellectual contribution of Darwinism outside biology itself was its demonstration that evolution could produce more sophisticated, and better adapted, organisms than could be created by design. But the analogy between biological evolution and socio-economic evolution should be treated only as an analogy. Adaptation in institutions and in economic life is not random, and the mechanisms of selection—the 'replicator dynamics'—are different. Since learning is important, social evolution is more Lamarckian than Darwinian.

If you believe in disciplined pluralism, you believe in the merits of experiment and appraisal, but you are not confident in market outcomes, and you certainly do not assume that they are efficient simply because they are market outcomes. You worry about the concentration of too much power in the hands of Microsoft, because it threatens pluralism. You don't see a problem if one leading City of London investment bank is acquired by an American firm; you do see a problem if all are. Decentralisation to local agencies will often be a means to pluralism, but it is not the same as pluralism, and local political control may be less pluralist than centralism. The requirements of pluralism would be better met by several autonomous state-owned hospital chains than by local monopolies of health care under local and singular political control. If you believe in pluralism you want central government to undertake small scale experiments—and you want it to be ready to acknowledge failure. This is very different from ideologically driven centralisation; rather, it is what Franklin Roosevelt, probably its greatest exponent, described as 'bold and persistent experimentation'.[3]

Incentive compatibility

The processes of disciplined pluralism are not necessarily fair. Priority in scientific ideas is often credited to the wrong person; the process of peer review often rejects the genuinely original. Only occasionally are pioneers in commercial innovation the leaders who build great businesses. In democratic elections voters need give no reasons for casting their votes, and there is no appeal against their verdict.

The absence of objective, transparent criteria in the discipline of markets in ideas, innovation and ideology is both disconcerting and important. But a requirement to lay down the basis of assessment in advance necessarily runs into problems of incentive compatibility: the common scourge of both socialism and regulated capitalism. To allocate scarce resources between competing ends—the central problem of any economic system—it is necessary to assess the scope of resources—what it is possible to produce—and the nature of ends—the requirements of firms and the wants and desires of consumers. But almost all this information has to be obtained from the various proponents of the competing ends.

How can they be persuaded to assess it diligently and reveal it accurately? Most people are honest and well intentioned, and if you ask them for information they will give it. But they may discover that doing so is not to their advantage. If targets are set and resources allocated on the basis of information revealed, then you will do better if you are conservative about what is possible, pessimistic about what is needed and optimistic about the benefits which will result from the adoption of your proposals. But the people to whom you supply the information will realise you are doing this, and calibrate their expectations accordingly. This process became known as 'plan bargaining' in socialist economies.[4]

No society in history offered such a wide range of rewards and punishments as the Soviet Union, from the economic and political privileges of the *nomenklatura* to the slave camps of the Gulag. The Soviet economic problem was not an absence of incentives: incentives to conform to the dictates of the centre were very strong. The Soviet economic problem was that the planners did not have good information on which to base their direction. It was on these twin problems of information and incentives that the Soviet economy foundered. And the information problem is the more fundamental. If a powerful state could accurately calibrate both abilities and needs, it could enforce production according to abilities and assignment according to needs. That is what the Soviet state sought, and failed, to do.

Plan bargaining is not confined to the Soviet Union, though it was endemic there. Plan bargaining is found in any system in which central authority must be locally implemented: in government regulation of business, in the control of public services, and in the management of large private sector organisations. When regulators supervise utilities, when governments set targets for schools and hospitals, they face the same problem: the information needed to determine the targets appropriately is held by people who are in electricity companies, in schools and hospitals, rather than government departments.

Lenin claimed to have found the answer to this problem: 'seize the decisive link'.[5] Because the information required to control the system completely is extensive and impossible to obtain, the centre must focus on a few supposedly key variables. But these are subject to 'Goodhart's Law'—'any observed regularity will tend to collapse when pressure is placed upon it for control purposes'.[6] If hospitals are judged by the number of people who wait more than twelve months for an operation, then the number of people who wait more than twelve months for an operation is likely to fall, but whether the service given to patients is better or worse is another matter altogether. If corporate executives receive bonuses related to earnings per share, then reported earnings per share may rise, but whether the business is better or more valuable is, again, a different question.

The inevitable consequence is the complication and proliferation of targets. These processes become confusing and inconsistent, and undermine the authority and morale of those who engage in the activities which are being planned. Incentive compatibility—the desire to provide information that will yield personal advancement rather than information that is true—undermines the process of rational decision making within the planning system itself. This is the common experience of large centralised organisations, public or private.

Regulated self-regulation

The fundamental problem of incentive compatibility—conflicting objectives combined with imprecise and distributed information—explains why the provision of public services, or the pursuit of social objectives, cannot be decentralised through a process of tightly defined contracts, except in narrow areas where outcomes can be precisely described and methods of achieving these outcomes are obvious and widely accepted, such as street cleaning or hospital laundries.

This view of contractualisation and decentralisation of public sector functions matches the experience of the private sector itself. General Motors would once distinguish sharply between customised components whose production the company must itself control, and commodity purchases which could safely be outsourced from the cheapest supplier; until Toyota demonstrated that better product quality, faster, leaner production, and more flexible response to changing market conditions could be achieved by looser trust relationships among a *keiretsu* of favoured suppliers.[7] The manufacture of complex products in a modern economy has become possible only by making permeable boundaries between firm and market. The delivery of complex services in a modern state will be possible only by making similarly permeable the boundaries between state and market.

The traditional distinction between policy and implementation is therefore one which, in economic matters, can rarely be made. The idea that the relationships between the state and other agents must be transparent, precisely defined, and non-discriminatory—which, for many people, still seems to be a fundamental requirement of public administration—is incompatible with the flexibility, innovation, discretion and judgement needed for the efficient delivery of services. Trust relationships are, necessarily, the product of social relationships in communities rather than legal structures.

This poses a challenging agenda. Informality and flexibility in commercial relationships between firms provide the real basis of innovation and change in the successful market economy, and government can match private sector innovation and change only through similar reform. This requires procedures oriented to outcome, not process. But how to achieve these results without opening the door to the corruption and arbitrariness which the legal regulation of relationships between the state and private sector is intended to prevent? The worst outcome—and a current danger—is to construct relationships between government and private firms which are formal in appearance but informal in substance: the extensively detailed contract is renegotiated, or set aside, whenever it comes under pressure from the inevitable occurrence of unpredicted events.

But the modern market economy functions effectively only because it is embedded in a social context. Relationships between state and market are therefore not simply, or mainly, matters of law, regulation and contract. The atmosphere in which they are conducted is critical. Economic policy is not simply, or primarily, a question of what the government should do. Government is simply one of the means by which the social context of the embedded market is expressed. Concepts such as reputation and legitimacy are equally important expressions of that context and play an equally central role in regulating economic activity.

So statutory regulation and self-regulation are not alternatives; in a properly functioning embedded market they are complementary. Law generally can only be enforced in a democratic society if it corresponds to the behaviour most people would engage in, or at least wish to see engaged in, anyway. And this is even more true of economic regulation, which cannot function by bullying recalcitrants into submission: its objectives are too complex, its subjects too sophisticated, for such mechanisms to be very effective. The collapses of Enron and WorldCom were reminders, if reminders were needed (they clearly were), that detailed prescriptive rules cannot constrain those who have no intention of being bound by their substance rather than their letter. When the young Alan Greenspan wrote that 'at the bottom of the endless pile of paperwork which characterises all regulation lies a gun',[8] he was talking nonsense: if economic regulation requires a gun for its enforcement, it will inevitably fail.

We cannot achieve truth in accounting reports or securities prospectuses by rules unless these rules are internalised by private business itself. Without elements of external regulation, self-regulation rapidly degenerates into self-congratulation—as it has in professions such as law, accountancy and medicine—but external regulation on its own can never fully secure the information or display the adaptability needed to achieve its purposes. In the financial services sector, as in others, the most powerful vehicle of regulation is mutually supportive reputation—respected traders deal only with respected traders, and confer that respect grudgingly. This mechanism was allowed to unwind in the last two decades when maximum greed within minimal rules became the credo of the market economy.

Conclusions

It is chastening that the experience of deliberate coordination of economic systems and of economic development demonstrated that such state coordination was generally worse than no coordination at all. The experience of economic planning under social democracy is no more encouraging, if perhaps less calamitous, than the experience of economic planning under communism. The fundamental, and intractable, problem is that such intervention presupposes knowledge of the economic system and economic environment which no one can validly claim to have. Claims to such knowledge are as empty when made by the visionary leaders of private businesses whose superior insights are confirmed by their large salaries as when they come from politicians whose unique appreciation of the course of future events is established by their victory at the ballot box. Those who do claim to have such knowledge are less worthy of our trust than those who recognise the limits of their understanding.

The correct lesson to draw is that the modern market economy, necessarily embedded in a social, political and cultural context, is a sensitive instrument whose functioning we understand only imperfectly. If the dismal experience of planned economies is illuminating, so is the dismal experience of New Zealand: the country which from 1984 to 1999 followed neo-liberal prescriptions more vigorously than any other developed economy, and enjoyed the worst macro-economic performance of any developed country over the same period.[9] The lesson of Soviet failure is not that the Marxist vision of economic organisation redesigned on entirely rationalist lines was the wrong vision, but that *any* attempt to implement grand economic designs is likely to end in failure.

Economic policy is properly subject- and context-specific. The institutions that are right for electricity generation are not the same as those which are right for water supply. The mechanisms of regulation appropriate for financial services are not the same as that for food retailing. But the key themes of this essay—the role of community in supporting economic life, the absence of a sharp distinction between the nature and functions of private and public business, the overriding requirement for disciplined pluralism in every area of economic life which involves the delivery of services, and the necessity of the interaction of rules and values—regulated self-regulation—in the control of economic activity—provide some general principles for the development of a political economy relevant to the governments of market economies for the twenty-first century.

Notes

1 This analysis is based on Chapters 8 and 9 of J. Kay, *The Truth about Markets*, London, Allen Lane, The Penguin Press, 2003.
2 The phrase comes from Edward Plowden, who for several decades epitomised the

rationalist view of relations between government and business in Britain; quoted in D. Henderson, 'Two British errors: their probable size and some possible reasons', *Oxford Economic Papers*, 1977, vol. 29, no. 2, pp. 159–205.

3 J. Rauch, *Demosclerosis: The Silent Killer of American Government*, New York, Random House, Times Books, 1994.

4 'Plan bargaining' is extensively described in J. Kornai, *The Socialist System*, Oxford, Oxford University Press, 1992.

5 See Kornai, *The Socialist System*.

6 C. Goodhart, *Monetary Theory and Practice: The UK Experience*, London, Macmillan, 1984.

7 K. Monteverdi and D. J. Teece, 'Supplier switching costs and vertical integration in the automobile industry', *Rand Journal of Economics*, 1982, pp. 206–13; J. P. Womack, D. T. Jones and D. Roos, *The Machine that Changed the World: The Story of Lean Production*, New York, HarperCollins, 1991.

8 Greenspan (1963) in A. Rand, *Capitalism: The Unknown Ideal*, New York, Signet, 1967.

9 T. Hazledine, *Taking New Zealand Seriously: The Economics of Decency*, Auckland, New Zealand, HarperCollins New Zealand Ltd, 1998.

Creating the Public Good

CHARLES LEADBEATER

THE BEST innovations often come from re-using old ideas. That is why the way that British cities created maps during their explosive nineteenth century growth might be a guide to how we should set about creating the public good more than a century later.[1]

British industrial cities, such as Manchester, grew as such a rate in the nineteenth century that they often outstripped the capacity of government to shape their growth. These cities were complex, self-organising and in the terminology of the complexity sciences, emergent. Cities exhibited an overall order despite their complexity, rapid growth and no one being in charge. Order, such as it was, appeared from within a largely self-organising but often chaotic system.

City maps were a social innovation to make this new collective space navigable for the millions of people drawn into cities from the countryside. The creation of maps was a massive, centrally orchestrated initiative, which required the state to gather far more information than it ever had before about city geography. It involved creating standardised, public rules for describing properties, spaces and roads. Before the advent of official maps, people had to navigate their way around using word of mouth and local knowledge. Maps did not just make this knowledge explicit. They created an entirely new public view of the world: they helped to constitute the city as a public realm. Maps were one of the devices new city dwellers had available to them to represent the public space they inhabited together.

Yet this constitution of the public also allowed a complementary expansion of private initiative and endeavour. Maps are not just a public representation of a shared reality. They are also a tool that people use, as individuals, to make their tracks across the city, to bend it to their ends. The map provided a public platform for a massive expansion of private activity. The two grew together.

The postal system was a similar innovation: a public platform for private endeavour. The Penny Post created in 1837 was made possible only by the state codifying information that for the first time systematically linked people, to their addresses and street names. All of that would have been impossible without public rules for gathering and representing information. The post created a new world of public information in which people could represent themselves and the state could identify them through their address, and in turn post code. Yet the constitution of this new world of public information also made possible a massive expansion in private activity: people in their millions took to letter writing. Public and private grew together. Much the same story might be told about the growth of libraries and sanitation: the

 Published by Blackwell Publishing Ltd, 9600 Garsington Road, Oxford OX4 2DQ, UK and 350 Main Street, Malden, MA 02148, USA

public realm created a platform for a massive expansion of private activity. People became clean not just because of public networks of sewers and water pipes but because—thanks to Lever's new-fangled bar of soap—they changed their personal habits: they started washing.

What lessons can we learn from these stories of how the state helped to create the public good amidst the social upheavals of the nineteenth century? A strict dividing line drawn between a 'public realm' and a 'private realm' is crude and misleading. Both the neo-liberal right and many on the centre left maintain the fiction of strict division between public and private. For the right, the public good expands as the state contracts, leaving greater room for private freedom and enterprise. For many on the centre left, the zero-sum calculation goes in the other direction: the state and public professionals embody the public good. The public good expands with their number and resources. Yet in all these cases—maps, postal systems, water and libraries—public and private grew together. The public realm was created in part to promote a complementary expansion of private activity, which in turn legitimated the investment in public goods. The connections between public and private go beyond that. In a sense, the liberal nineteenth century state governed through freedom: it recognised it had to create order in society by influencing how people exercised their private choices. The public good can only be created if its values infiltrate deep into the private domain. A public realm defensively walled off in its cherished institutions and professional disciplines would be incapable of infiltrating deeply into civil society. Only a state that governs through freedom, by shaping how people make private choices, can do so. That too is the task of the modern state. The modern British state, not just in cities but across most of its domain, has to rule through freedom, not against it.

Government is an unfolding act of improvisation, trying to create public goods, juggling with inherited materials that were designed for different tasks in earlier eras, and conducted mainly in poor light but in front of a massive audience that can, at any time, swing its searchlight onto you.

The chief challenge facing government in a liberal, open society is how to help create public goods—like a well educated population with an appetite to learn, or a healthy society without appetites for fatty foods—in a society with a democratic ethos, which prizes individual freedom and wants to be self-organising and 'bottom–up'.

Even within the 'public domain' the government is dealing with a highly complex system. In education, for example, 'the government' at the centre is a many headed hydra with many thousands of civil servants spread across the DfES, the QCA and Ofsted. They in turn deal with many people who do not work for the government but many different governments and governors: hundreds of LEAs, thousands of schools, many more heads, teachers, and governors. Beyond them lie a range of suppliers of textbooks, technology and other services, and millions of children and their parents. Attitudes towards learning are strongly influenced by family background and peer pressure.

Influencing decisions parents and children take at home, in their living rooms and bedrooms, over how they spend their leisure time will be as critical in producing the public good as employing more, better trained teachers.

The public good—a society that values and provides for education—will only emerge from millions of interconnected decisions, many of them taken outside the school system, influenced by factors beyond the direct control of teachers, let alone government ministers.

This poses questions that are not just about the techniques and levers government might use to get its job done. It is far more fundamental: what is the role of government in a society that wants to be self-organising? What is the role of the state in managing these complex systems, in which the government can only achieve its goals by working through and with people it cannot control and who will reject state intrusion into their lives?

It is a question that modern British politics has been trying to answer at least since 1979, when Mrs Thatcher arrived with her neo-liberal answer to that question. When Labour came to power in 1997 it did not have a clear answer. It improvised one by building upon what seemed to work in practice during its first term: a powerful central drive to make the state machine more effective at delivering what users wanted. Now as the limitations of that approach become apparent, we are entering another phase. Could a mixture of reformed centralism to allow more earned autonomy and new localism to provide greater local say over services and personalisation, to give users more voice and choice over their services, provide the basis for another, perhaps more durable answer to how the state creates public goods in an open, liberal society?

Government cannot decide on its definition of the public good and impose it from above, at least not continually—witness the poll tax and the furore over tuition fees. But neither can the state afford to stand back and see what emerges from complex, self-organising systems, like education and health, in which there are lots of players with degrees of autonomy. Left to its own devices any self-organising system is likely to create chaos or stasis as well as dynamism and innovation. The British secondary education system left to its own self-organising devices would probably entrench under-achievement and low aspirations, as well as provide some with greater opportunities for learning.

So, in the name of equity, the centre of government has to exert a powerful influence over how a system like education or health operates. Yet how do the strategies and plans dreamt up in Whitehall get translated into decisions by thousands of heads, tens of thousands of teachers and millions of children and parents? As the centre becomes frustrated that its plans seem to get 'lost in translation', so it tries to compensate by enforcing them more strictly, only exacerbating the friction in the system.

Yet most of the work of government is not conducted in departments in Whitehall but at thousands of points scattered across society. In an open, self-organising society government has to become molecular: it has to get into the bloodstream of society, not try to impose change from without. Government is exercised in a myriad of micro settings, and often not just by state employees but by teachers, experts, advisers, parents, volunteers, peers. Shaping their activity and the influence they have on the people they serve is critical.

The challenge the central state faces—which the vogue for new localism only gestures at—is to shift from a model in which the centre controls, initiates, plans, instructs, to one in which the centre governs through promoting collaborative, critical and honest self-evaluation and improvement. The centre should not try to drive the public sector like an engine powering a car. It should instead seek to make sure the public sector is increasingly able to drive and police itself, and in the process help to create platforms for expanding private choice and initiative.

Neo-liberalism to New Labour

The neo-liberal answer to how the state should govern a self-organising society was deceptively and appealingly simple. The top–down organisation of the state had to be reduced as far as possible, limited to enforcing the law, providing defence and protecting freedom. That would allow the public good to emerge, bottom–up, from a free society, with a vibrant market and widely spread private property. As Mrs Thatcher put it: 'We need a strong state to preserve both liberty and order but we should not expect the state to appear in the guise of an extravagant good fairy at every christening, a loquacious and tedious companion at every stage of life's journey, the unknown mourner at every funeral.'

The neo-liberal approach ran into the sand because of the tensions inherent in it. The state had to act decisively, even in an authoritarian manner, to create the conditions for bottom–up freedom, even going so far as imposing the poll tax and other controversial measures by which it defined the public good.

New Labour was elected with a vague yet emotionally powerful mandate to recuperate the role of government to bind society together. New Labour initially toyed with ideas of community, mutuality and the third sector as the embodiments of how public good could bubble up almost voluntarily from below. Those early ideas, and the organisations that seemed to embody them, proved too fragile to sustain the weight put upon them. So from the middle of 2000 the government decisively shifted towards public service reform as the way to better align a top–down state with the demands of a bottom–up society. The recipe would be to invest and reform public services to help deliver improvements in education, health and other services that people demanded.

The basic message was that a top–down state could be made more legitimate only by becoming far more effective at delivering services to users. That would mean the centre driving change by setting stretching targets. Layers of government and external suppliers signed service level agreements to deliver to specific targets. External inspectors were on hand to drive quality and league tables to provided users with more information about service performance. The apparent success of the first term literacy and numeracy strategy, driven from the centre, was taken as a model for other services. New Labour's approach came from a mixture of management theory, ideas borrowed from the private sector and generalising from what appeared to be its outstanding domestic first term success.

Education was at the forefront of this approach. The secondary education system left to its own devices had become self-organising but non-adaptive. Low aspirations and ambitions were not challenged. Bad performance was not rooted out. Innovations were not spread. Under-performance was allowed to drift. The answer seemed to be to turn it into something more like a well run machine, in which instructions and energy imparted from the centre was more likely to get translated into action on the ground. Ministers needed a 'transmission belt' to carry policy into practice.

It is worth dwelling on the value of this centralised approach, especially at a time when decentralisation is all the rage. The centre needs to provide challenge and ambition for the system as a whole. Without that, there is a danger that local providers will just slip into local equilibrium, finding their own local 'fitness peak' but not aiming higher. Improvement depends on common yardsticks and measures of performance. (A chief feature of modern self-organising collectives—the Linux software community and the auction system eBay with its 30 million members, for example—is that they thrive on clear, simple and trustworthy information about performance.) The centre can play a vital role in establishing this common currency, acting like a central bank. The centre's role will be vital for equity. Infantile new localism, on its own, will not help the least able and less well equipped. Self-organisation in education has tended to help the better off, those most able to take opportunities. The centre has to act as a corrective to the tendencies for the knowledge and learning rich to becoming richer and the knowledge and learning poor to become poorer.

The limits of public service reform

The downsides of this centrally driven top–down initiative approach are by now widely accepted. The centre of government seems to have grown in size and become unwieldy, with departments jostling with semi-autonomous regulators to gain the attention of Number 10 and the Treasury. As any parent who has run a child's birthday party knows, demands for attention will go up to meet the available supply of parents. It works the other way too: the only way an overstaffed centre can legitimise its activities is by getting over-involved in the day-to-day running of services. This multi-centre sees its job to be to act upon the rest of the system, as an external force. This has helped to create an adversarial culture in which the centre insists and the rest of the system resists. That has fed growing complaints about the scale of teachers' workloads, conflicting targets, the anxiety bred by the inspection process, disputes about the veracity of league tables. As front line morale falls so it becomes even harder for the centre to make sure its directives are translated into action.

Accountability always flows upwards. Who is held responsible for the failure of London's tube system in 2003? Not the London Mayor but the transport department. Everyone looks up for funding, guidance and permission. Command and control is as much a mindset as a system. It is a mindset in which practitioners automatically look up for approval and permission even when they do not need central approval. Too many good ideas for public services improvement are 'trapped on location' in local offices, schools and hospitals. The public sector does not have an innovation problem. New ideas and services are being created the whole time. Public services are bedevilled by poor diffusion and propagation of innovations. Good ideas do not spread fast enough, and one reason for that is that a system that relies on the centre to gather, distil and propagate innovation will learn too slowly.

That failure to diffuse good ideas fast enough (and by implication to drive out bad ones) is one reason why the top–down approach is delivering diminishing returns. Services might be improving in line with increased inputs and resources, but there has been no step change in performance within the system, even during the 'fat years' of Gordon Brown's public spending spree. That is clear in many aspects of education, where rates of improvement in key indicators have begun to plateau.

Perhaps the biggest problem with this managerialist approach is the way it conflates 'delivery of public services' with the 'creation of the public good'. In many areas—education, smoking, obesity, the environment, community safety—the public good will only emerge from millions of individual decisions, each taken in their micro-locales, which combine to create the public good. These complex public goods cannot be delivered; they have to be created from within society. Public services can play a vital role in enabling this creative activity. Government plays a wider role in fostering the conditions for people to create public goods—through regulation, information campaigns, taxation and other tools.

However the language of the capable, effective, problem solving state creates the impression that public services can alone resolve complex social issues. The reality is that public services can provide a platform on which the public good is created, but public services are rarely, on their own, the total solution. Better policing rarely makes an estate safer on its own. It can make a vital contribution but so do a myriad of initiatives on anti-social behaviour, community safety, lighting, recreational activities, traffic calming and even landscaping. Better teaching can make a huge difference to how children learn. But the value of teaching is amplified many times over by what happens at home and amongst friends and peers. The value of a BBC programme is multiplied many times over if there are routes—magazines, websites, courses, clubs—through which people can develop the interests sparked by the programme.

Labour's approach since 2000 has been to take a system that was regarded as self-organising but rather ramshackle and to turn it into more of a machine, which could deliver more predictable, controlled results. The sustained criticism of this top–down approach has brought us to a choice over the way ahead.

One response to the growing criticism of the heavy handed top–down approach is to try to create a more reliable, fine-tuned machine, one that runs with less friction, consumes less fuel and produces less pollution. That would try to contain the system's self-organising features but do so more intelligently and selectively. Another answer would be to recognise that public goods like education and health emerge from the way that public services interact with wider society, triggering and sustaining a process in which public goods develop within civil society.

Reformed centralism, new localism and personalisation

There are three main strands in current attempts to make the state more responsive and adaptive in how it delivers public services and so helps to create the public good.

The first main strand has come from the government itself: reformed and intelligent centralism. The top–down model of public service delivery can be reformed to make it less heavy handed and so more responsive to bottom–up initiatives and demand. Earned autonomy for schools and hospitals grants players a conditional right to be self-organising, dependent on their continued good performance. Specialist status creates greater diversity of supply. A new compact with the professions in health and education is aimed at increasing recruitment, reducing workload, creating a new division of labour with para-professionals and allowing greater scope for professional judgement in the classroom.

A second strand is new localism. Distrust of centralised initiatives makes a shift towards local decision making over priorities and funding more attractive, despite the poor esteem in which a lot of local government is held and the patchiness of local capacity. (The council tax revolt among pensioners in early 2004 showed that many people do not think local services are necessarily better, nor that local government is that much closer to the people.) New localism speaks to a desire for greater self-government from a more bottom–up world. Accountability for local issues—such as transport and schooling—would not flow upwards to departments and ministers as they would be increasingly handled locally. That dispersion of accountability and responsibility would make life more manageable for a central state that is overloaded with demands upon it.

The third strand is personalisation: public services will gather more support by being more response to individual needs. The top–down state too often delivers 'one size fits all' services; personalisation would give users more say in what kind of service they wanted, where, when and how. In education this would allow children and parents more choice over their routes through the system, their curriculum, style and pace of learning, mode of assessment.

When they are combined, these three strands will create a variable geometry public sector with far greater diversity of institutions, governance arrangements at local level, curricula, assessment techniques and funding formulas.

New localism, almost by definition, cannot be imposed from the centre. It has to arise from local demand. But then that means localities will move at different speeds towards different definitions of greater local autonomy. What that autonomy means will differ from Birmingham, where the council is giving neighbourhoods greater power in the name of bottom–up involvement, to Tower Hamlets, where they are re-centralising services because neighbourhood organisations have led to wasteful duplication. In some areas—such as Gateshead, home to one of the most improved LEAs in the country—new localism will mean the local authority having more power. In other areas it could be the local strategic partnership or other as yet unimagined governance arrangements. But new localism is just one version of an accommodation with a more 'bottom–up' and self-organising world. Personalisation could lead towards more direct decision making by parents and children, rather than by local politicians. Meanwhile, reformed centralism will create its own devolved institutions—semi-autonomous, licensed providers including specialist schools, foundation hospitals and their federations—which may have quite different governance arrangements from those of a revived new localism.

Top–down, bottom–up public services

In a liberal open society, government cannot deliver public goods nor can it instruct them to be created. Nor can a centre-left government stand back and accept whatever emerges from a self-organising society, because we know that could all too easily lead to under-achievement and deepen inequity.

The solution is that government can only promote the creation of public goods—like education and health—by influencing decisions taken by millions of private individuals. The government is committed to protecting the private sphere and self-governance but simultaneously committed to shaping the decisions made by autonomous agents. It cannot instruct autonomous agents, but neither can it afford to be neutral about what they do.

Government then is not just about providing services, nor even about making regulations. It is an endeavour to shape the conduct of people in their private lives as parents, teachers, students, taxpayers. Government is about shaping freedom; getting people to exercise choices in a collectively responsible way. Yet of course many people—teachers, parents, kids—question the central state's authority to tell them anything about how they should live their lives. The state increasingly has to act through intermediaries, experts, third parties to relay and translate its strategies into action.

That means government should increasingly be about creating spaces in which responsible self-regulation can be exercised; promoting the common yardsticks and measures against which people judge themselves; making sure information is open, transparent, shared, trustworthy; providing some clear goals and values for the system as a whole; encouraging collaborative self-evaluation, self-regulation and self-improvement among providers as the driving force of the system.

What would that mean for the division of labour within public services? At its heart would be a simple deal. Freedom from central control comes at a price. The price is far more effective, robust measures to promote collective self-regulation, self-evaluation and improvement. That will depend on open, honest, agreed measures of performance; decisive action from within the system to tackle under-performance; better systems for creating and propagating new ideas laterally, to spread best practice rather than just drive it from the centre. Those pressing for greater self-regulation can have it *only if* they accept the responsibilities and accountabilities that implies. Self-organising, adaptive communities work only by being uncompromising self-regulators.

What would that mean for the role of the centre of government? Its role would be as the architect of a system like education—deciding on its overall shape, who the main players are, and the interfaces between them. It would also be a platform provider: it would provide the platform of infrastructure, rules, information systems and performance measures to ensure the system as a whole works. The centre would set simple goals and boundaries—about equity and inclusion, international benchmarks—that would continue to challenge the system as a whole to improve.

A chasm has opened up between people and large organisations, both public and private. Many people's experience of being a consumer is that they are put on hold, kept at arm's length, not told the whole story, tricked by the fine print, redirected to a website and treated like a number. We feel detached from large organisations, public and private, that serve us in increasingly impersonal ways. While choice among commodity goods and services has expanded, the scope for personalised, human service, tailored to your needs, seems to have declined.

This gap between large organisations and the intricacy of people's everyday expectations and aspirations is a breeding ground for a growing sense of frustration and resentment, with private services as much as public. This chasm should also be the breeding ground for innovation and experimentation. The debate about the future of public services is pitched into this chasm between the way public institutions work and how users experience them. Targets, league tables and inspection regimes may have improved aspects of performance in public services. Yet the cost has been to make public services seem more machine-like, more like a production line producing standardised goods.

Across a range of activities it is increasingly clear that the state cannot deliver collective solutions from on high. It is too cumbersome and distant. The state can only help create public goods—like better education and health—by encouraging them to emerge from within society.

In health, for example, outcomes depend heavily on the lifestyle and behaviour of citizens (diet, exercise, smoking, drinking) and only modestly on the quality of hospital care. The Wanless review of the future of the NHS found that the key variable that would determine the health of the British population was not the number of doctors, but the way that patients and the public adapted their behaviour to make themselves healthier through exercise, diet and abstaining from smoking. Home-based self-management of long term conditions—diabetes, heart conditions—will be vital in an ageing society.

Crime and antisocial behaviour is strongly affected by the values and behaviour of individuals, families and communities, while only modestly affected by the activities of the police and courts. In education, research suggests that most of the variation in educational outcomes is explained by what happens at home as much as by what happens at school. More sustainable use of resources depends on changes in consumer behaviour through energy efficiency, recycling and re-use. The tax system increasingly depends on mass involvement in self-assessment and reporting. Three million people in Britain are seriously under-providing for their pension, and between 5 million and 10 million more are not saving enough. The state cannot change their behaviour through diktat nor through a public service alone, a better state pension. A collective solution to pensions provision will require self-regulation, new products and services and millions of people being encouraged to choose different ways to save for the future. Welfare to work and active labour market programmes are premised on the user as an active participant who takes responsibility for building up their skills and contacts. Neighbourhood renewal has to come from within; it cannot be delivered top–down from the state. Most community regeneration pro-grammes now involve local residents as participants in the process—design-ing and delivering change. Home care services are increasingly designed to encourage and enable elderly people to stand on their own two feet, cook, clean and look after themselves rather than to provide them with a long term service.

Public policy is most effective when it harnesses and shapes private activity rather than supplants it, allowing the public good to emerge from private initiative within civil society. The state's job will be to orchestrate and enable that process, not to pretend it can provide or deliver solutions in the form of discrete services.

In some areas the onus will be on changes to private behaviour which cumulatively create public value. No public infrastructure or dedicated institutions may be involved. Anti-smoking policy is a good example. Smoking causes about a third of all cancer, about one-sixth of heart and circulatory disease and more than 80% of serious lung disease. It costs the NHS more than £1,500 million a year to treat smoking related diseases. The indirect social costs of smoking—lost productivity, pain, loss and harm to non-smokers—has never been established. About 83% of smokers say they would not smoke if they could have their time again. Promoting smoking cessation is a clear public good. Public policy plays a critical role in making smoking unattractive—through increased taxation, anti-smoking campaigns, restricting advertising, public information and courses that help people to stop smoking. Public policy is in direct conflict with commercial interests which promote smoking at the cost of wider society. Yet smoking cessation cannot be delivered like a takeaway pizza or created at the instructions of professionals such as teachers and doctors. The public good—fewer people smoking—will come about through millions of individual decisions. The public good will be built bottom–up. It will come from public values and norms infiltrating private decision making. The public good—a society in which far fewer people smoke—will not exist in a distinct 'public realm'; it will only be created from within the private realm of the market.

The state will be a vital actor in creating the public good of a low-smoking nation. Smoking is declining fastest amongst the most well off and better educated: these are the people who are more likely to have the information, incentives and resources to change their lives. In contrast, 70% of single mothers smoke. The capacity to make these lifestyle choices are unequally distributed; so too are the outcomes. Poor and poorly educated people smoke; well-off and well educated people do not.

The English state in particular is caught in a bind: committed to protecting, even expanding, the sphere of private freedom it is also necessarily committed to shaping how people exercise their freedom. In social democratic countries—Finland is an outstanding example—the state and society seemed to be fused through a wide array of institutions that ensure consensus and cohesion. Top-down and bottom-up work together through a dense mix of institutions that calibrate how people act within the public and private sphere. Yet in England certainly, and the rest of Britain probably, the state has to act through freedom. In the name of equity it cannot stand aside and accept what the self-organising rhythms of an unequal society throw up: that would just be more and deeper inequality. But in a society which also prizes freedom and autonomy that means the state has to rule through the rhetoric of freedom, even when the goal is to enhance equity and deepen the public good. That is the tension the modern British state seems to be built on. It shows no sign of easing.

Note

1 This essay has drawn upon many sources, including: Gavin Kelly and Stephen Meuers, *Creating Public Value: An Analytical Framework for Public Service Reform*, Strategy Unit, Cabinet Office, www.strategy.gov.uk; Jim Maxmin and Shoshana Zuboff, *The Support Economy*, Penguin, 2003; Patrick Joyce, *The Rule of Freedom*, Verso, 2003; and Nikolas Rose, *The Powers of Freedom*, Cambridge University Press, 2003.

The State and Innovations in Economic Governance

COLIN CROUCH

MY MAIN purpose in this chapter is to go beyond the polemical dichotomy of 'state versus market', and to set both within a wider framework of several different modes of governance, which come together in varying combinations. I want to show how appreciation of the diversity of these modes enables us to see a broad range of institutional possibilities with which governments and others can experiment in economic policy. Achievement of this kind of diversity was part of the reformulation of social democracy for a post-Fordist, post-industrial society promised by Third Way thinkers during the late 1990s. In practice, the British New Labour government has been inhibited from exploring the possibilities of this diversity by its increasingly dogmatic commitment to the market as its single preferred mode of governance.

A striking example may be taken from recent comments on the British National Health Service by Julian Le Grand, now a central figure in government policy in this area. Initially, he was unable to distinguish governance of the NHS and similar social democratic institutions from the mechanisms of the Soviet state.[1] In the later of the two contributions cited, he explicitly moderates this view (pp. 48–50), but in a significant way. He acknowledges a major role for what he calls 'networks and trust' alongside 'command and control' in the NHS. But he then identifies networks and trust with subordination to the judgement of public service professionals. The overall aim of his argument is then to advocate the role of markets as the sole reliable approach to public service. Therefore it is not just the state but all other non-market forms of governance which need to be viewed negatively.

Highly paradoxically, this same commitment to the market has also led New Labour to be very state-centric, further constraining its capacity to encourage diversity. It is important to address this particular paradox at an early stage. It can be done by way of dealing with another currently popular dichotomy, which appears whenever one discusses governance: that between government and governance. Many observers are suspicious of this, seeing in 'governance' an unnecessary grandiloquence on the part of those who find 'government' simply too straightforward. (Harold Wilson is often seen as the start of the problem by these observers, when he called his autobiography *The Governance of Britain* though he was in fact just talking about government.[2]) Against them, two different groups see substantive meaning in the distinction. I share the critical stance against the first of these, but not the second.

 Published by Blackwell Publishing Ltd, 9600 Garsington Road, Oxford OX4 2DQ, UK and 350 Main Street, Malden, MA 02148, USA

Problems of the Third Way approach to governance

The first group contrast government and governance by seeing the former as hard-edged, rigid and rather nasty, and the latter as soft, flexible, and responsive. For example, Leach and Percy-Smith[3] associate 'old government' with 'command and control', 'hierarchy and authority', 'institutions and organisational structures'. 'New governance', however, is associated with, respectively, 'facilitating, collaborating, and bargaining', 'networks and partnerships', 'processes, policies, outputs and outcomes'. Those who are surprised to learn from this that old government had no policies, and that new governance manages without any institutions, may then be mystified to discover that old government 'rows' while new governance 'steers'.[4] This deconstructionist, postmodernist vision of a future, in which firm institutions vanish into thin air, was very much part of the early Third Way or New Labour interpretation of its own divergence from social democracy. As Anthony Giddens expressed it, in social democracy the state was pervasive and dominated over civil society.[5] The Third Way state, in contrast, would be benign: it was 'the state without enemies', 'doubly' democratic, transparent, working in partnership with civil society and harnessing local initiatives.[6]

These are all clear, coherent arguments, and there is a nugget of truth somewhere in them. But they make strange reading after several years of a New Labour government that has been secretive, centralising, at least as reliant as its Old Labour and Conservative predecessors on exclusive cliques of insiders, and also determinedly military. There are strong reasons why the Third Way project has not seen the state deconstruct itself into a non-coercive type of governance; and these need to be understood.

First, whatever changes are made to the forms of government and its interventions in economy and society, at the centre lies the fact of political power, possession of and closeness to which always bring reward and privilege. The mid-twentieth century Keynesian welfare state was distinguished from other forms by the broad, even universal, swathes of population able to share in the state's capacity to provide benefits, not by the phenomenon of state benefit itself. Political power and influence remain objects of struggle just as intensely when the social state declines; it is just that the circles involved in political struggle and its fruits become more limited. Elites will always remain vitally interested in the state, as they will be served first by whatever is available. Business sectors, individual firms, and other groups able to achieve personal access to officers of state continue to lobby, whatever the general role of government in society. If the early twenty-first century US neo-conservative polity represents some kind of paradigm case of the new residual state, it is certainly not one where business interests consider that government has become so limited that there is little need to seek access to it. And US politicians continue to seek vast corporate donations to help their campaigns. If anything, this has grown as the welfare state has declined.

Second, as Andrew Gamble demonstrated early during the neo-liberal Thatcher years, producing the 'free economy' *required* a 'strong state'—in particular a strong central one.[7] To the extent that New Labour stands for a continuation of the market-making agenda, it is subject to the same logic.

There are highly important historical precedents for the dependence of the free economy on the strong state. The original emergence of capitalism out of medieval political economy had involved a similar process. The premodern polity had been at least as complex as any image of early twenty-first century governance. The emperor, kings, local nobility, professional corporations, towns, church authorities, all laid claim to different elements of political power, and to different interventions in economic behaviour. Capitalism developed most easily when this rich diversity had been simplified following the emergence of sovereign nation-states, which gathered this parcelised sovereignty into themselves. Thus simplified, it was necessary to convince only this one authority in a given national territory to accept a limited role for political intervention and to provide and guarantee the conditions for free markets and enforceable contracts.

When the UK embarked on its second capitalist revolution in the 1980s, something similar occurred. The strong central state weakened the scope of local government and intermediate associations (mainly the social partner organisations), as well as the European Union from above, in order to construct space for a free economy. *Pace* Leach and Percy-Smith, it had in fact been 'old government', at least though not solely in its social democratic form, that had thrived on bargaining and compromise; it was the 'new governance' of neo-liberalism that fought against such arrangements in order to clarify and purify market forces.

In the 1980s British neo-liberals did not deny Gamble's observations; but— like the Bolsheviks after the 1917 Russian Revolution—they believed that the strong state was a temporary necessity, needed to clean out the accretions of social democracy. Once that had been achieved, free markets would blossom and the strong state could wither away. They were naive. First, they forgot that people like to enjoy political power for purposes other than liberalising economies, and concentrated power is even more enjoyable as well as less vulnerable to checks and balances than dispersed power and compromises. Second, they believed that the creation of markets was somehow a once-and-for-all-time activity.

Now, a quarter of a century later, we know that neo-liberal governments keep finding it necessary to take new initiatives to keep markets pure and extend their scope. This is partly because dynamic, sophisticated economies present an endless stream of issues that require attention and that cannot simply be read off from some free-market calculus. For example, there is no once-and-for-all judgement on how far technological innovation requires protection of copyright and patent, and how far it needs open competition. The balance achieved at any one moment is a political one, and liable to change and to require adjustment as politics and technology change. To take a different example: if entrepreneurs are constantly seeking new ways of making profit, they will find ever new ways of evading laws, including those designed to guarantee free markets. The market-protecting state has to be constantly vigilant against them. Those seeking profit-maximisation will do so through the tough road of true market competition only if there is no alternative. It is far easier to make profit through rent-seeking, monopolistic practice, political dealing and corruption. These alternatives will not only be used; they will be forged anew in response to the most recent cycle of pro-market regulation, in an indefinitely repeating cycle.

The market economy does not exist in some state of nature, to which we all naturally turn unless the state inhibits us. Those who believed that the collapse of the Soviet system was all that was needed to release the 'natural' capitalist instincts of the people of Russia and Eastern Europe were distressed to find that mafia rather than markets flourished. Thomas Hobbes was right about the state of nature after all. Human nature may well be acquisitive and maximising, but it requires the construction of highly elaborate and con-straining rules and powerful, deliberately constructed institutions to channel that acquisitiveness into buying and selling goods, investing in stock markets, establishing companies according to specific legal codes.

We have to be directed and shaped to make us pursue our goals through market means alone. Although it is often defined in terms of its offer of freedom of choice, the market offers only choices of certain kinds. Before we participate in markets we have to be disciplined so that we use its means and no others. This is not only the case in the struggle against corruption. People often also seek to protect areas of their life from the market: for example, their religious practices, their leisure time, or their citizenship rights. One way of seeing the political struggles of at least the past two centuries is as continuing dispute over where this line should be drawn. From the point of view of business interests, the more areas of life that can be drawn within the scope of commodification and sale on the market, the more scope there is for profit. But they need the state, not only to open the market route, but also to prohibit or make difficult non-market means of achieving the same ends. This is the issue behind contemporary debates over the commercialisation of public services, such as the growth of private health care and student tuition fees. If these areas of life are to be opened to the market, the population must be drawn away from existing concepts of citizenship rights in these areas.[8] The introduction of the market into an area where it did not exist before is not a liberation from constraints, but a replacement of one kind of constraint by another.

Neo-liberalism, neo-conservatism, and New Labourism—all versions of the market-making state—produce, despite their rhetoric, very busy, tough and demanding governments. Such a state cannot risk the compromises and bargaining that were meat and drink to the social and Christian democracy and old liberalism of the mid- to late twentieth century; its task is to purify and restore markets, not to make compromises between them and non-market forces. For example, negative and positive incentives have to be designed to persuade increasing proportions of the population to enter the labour force; it must be made absolutely clear to able-bodied adults that they can have a life free of poverty only if they work, and not necessarily even then. There is nothing soft and furry about the new governance of the market-making state.

The security state

More important still, in at least its US and British manifestations, the new rolled back form of the state has been associated with a return to prominence of the hardest, most centralised, least compromising, as well as the oldest, of all forms of state action: war. And alongside the new role of external security—and closely linked to it by xenophobia and real fear of terror-ism—appears the new internal security agenda: strong policing, diminished civil rights. It is here that neo-liberalism passes into neo-conservatism. What are we to make of the fact that the two advanced nations that have gone furthest down the road of neo-liberal reform are also the two that have gone furthest in reasserting the role of military force in resolving international disputes? Also, at least within Europe, governments are more likely to support the new Anglo-American security strategy the closer they are to free-market economic policies.

Is there a connection here, or is it just coincidence? There are several reasons for believing that there may be some link. First, in both the neo-liberal and the new security agendas there is a renunciation of two postwar traditions: first, the treatment of compromise as virtue; second, acceptance of regulation. With respect to the latter, the refusal of the Bush administration in the USA to accept international rules closely resembles the rejection of regulation by corporations, and sometimes involves the same issues. Further, market-making is not entirely absent from the Anglo-American military project. One of its aims is to force reluctant elites to enter the world of capitalist trade—just as the US fleet had done to Japan in the 1850s.

There may also be a connection between the rise of the warfare state and the decline of the welfare state. History has given us only two models of how democratic nation states secure the loyalty of mass populations: solidarity in the face of external enemies; and identification with extensive rights of social citizenship. From the end of the Second World War onwards, all advanced democracies based themselves on extensive citizenship rights and, within the context of the Cold War and the fear of nuclear annihilation, turned their backs on the use of warfare as a means of reinforcing social solidarity. Since the 1980s the USA and the UK have taken the lead in constructing the post-welfare state. This leaves them vulnerable to popular disenchantment and apathy. Appeals to solidarity in the face of both internal and external threats to the homeland might provide a functional substitute. None of this was foreseen by those who saw the move away from social democratic government as one towards soft and gentle governance.

The social science approach to governance

The second group of writers who see purpose in distinguishing government from governance have a more scientific than political agenda. This approach treats government as a *subset* of governance, one form that governance can take. For this second approach to talk of a move 'from government to governance' makes sense only as a move 'from government *to other types of governance*'; though, as we shall see, as a statement of historical tendency this too is problematic.

Governance is best understood as: *all means by which the behavioural regularities that constitute social institutions are maintained and enforced*. Social institutions are then to be defined as: *clusters of patterns of action and relationships which continue and reproduce themselves over time, independently of the identity of the biological individuals performing within them*. This basic idea can be applied to institutions of very different sizes and degrees of formality, from the family to certain international structures. It therefore provides a means of considering real diversity.

Government as such is clearly included within the scope of governance seen in this way, but there are also other forms, which must be considered alongside it and compared with it. Those that are mainly considered in the literature are the market, associations, communities, networks and corporate hierarchies.[9] It is also important to distinguish between the state as government in its direct, interventionist, taxing and spending role, on the one hand; and the state as the source and guarantor of formal law, on the other.[10]

In reality, these different modes of governance appear alone very rarely indeed; they are almost always found in various combinations. This characteristic is fundamental to the whole argument of this chapter, and I shall return to it. However, temporarily, and just in order to gain an understanding of the differences among them, let us look at the different modes as though they were a series of pure forms.

The substantive state The ideal, in the sense of pure or extreme, concept of substantive state governance is one in which its central command capacity shapes the entire environment. All resources are provided through the state, which allocates them through its administrative structure. Resources have low mobility, because change requires application to the administration. Communication is through the signalling of requests and commands; the state is not here defined as a necessarily democratic one, but simply as a state, working through a centralised and potentially coercive structure. These processes are formal; relations are vertical; and the state has in principle a high capacity for enforcement, with an extensive and general reach. When and if they ever operated according to their basic principles, the state socialist economies of the former Soviet bloc worked something like this.

The association In the pure concept of an associational economy, all firms and individuals are members of formal organisations, which are responsible for all their relations with the external environment. Resources are all channelled through associations' administrative structure. Resources have low mobility, because change requires application to the association. Communication is through dialogue, because associations are defined as membership organisations. These processes are formal; relations are vertical; and the association has in principle a high capacity for enforcement among its members, but its reach is not general. The guild economies of medieval Europe functioned partly, but only partly, according to this model. Associational governance is widespread in advanced economies, especially in Western Europe, but never appears alone. The association differs from the state in that it has an internal dialogue structure and limited external reach.

The community In a pure community, individuals are strongly embedded in informal and usually local and enduring, multiply interlocking webs of relationships, which also govern all their contacts with the external environment. All resources come from the community, which allocates them through custom and tradition. Resources have low mobility, because they are embedded in the community. Communication is through dialogue, because communities are defined as membership structures. These processes are informal; relations are horizontal; and, through the interlocking nature of its relationships, the community has a high capacity for enforcement among its members. However, its reach beyond the community is not extensive. Many subsistence peasant economies functioned according to this model. The community differs from the association in the informality of its procedures, and the horizontal character of its relations.

The network In a network (as in a network economy), individual units are linked loosely with each other in limited understandings concerning reciprocity. Resources are provided by the network, which allocates them through its structures. Resources have high mobility, because the binding undertakings of the network are weak. Communication is through dialogue, because networks are defined as membership structures. These processes can be either formal or informal, giving us two subtypes. In the former case, there is an explicit agreement among the members concerning the inception, conduct and conclusion of the network; in the latter, understandings develop in a similar way as in community, but always in a more limited and less embedded way. In both forms, relations are horizontal; and the network has a low capacity for enforcement among its members, because their relations are weak. It also has no reach beyond the members. Arrangements among small numbers of multinational firms to develop new products together, as described by Ohmae,[11] would be examples of networks of the formal kind—though always found alongside other governance modes. The web of production facilities, research sites, universities, legal specialists and sector-specific venture capitalists clustered around the so-called 'Silicon Valley' zone of California is an instance of informal but still powerful networks—again always alongside other modes.[12] The network differs from the community in the partial and superficial character of the bonds that link its members.

The market In the pure concept of a neo-classical market economy, firms and individuals are linked to each other and to resources and factors of production solely by relations of supply and demand as signalled by price under conditions of perfect competition. All resources are acquired in the market, through purchase. Resources have high mobility, because they respond solely to price signals. Communication is solely through these signals; participants in the market are anonymous and therefore cannot participate in dialogue. Processes are formal, because calculations have to be precise for the market to work efficiently. Relations are horizontal; and the market has a low capacity for autonomous enforcement because of the criterion of anonymity. However, if its functioning can be guaranteed, its reach is extensive, all transactions being in principle commensurable. The market differs from the network in its dependence on price rather than allocation as its mode of acquisition of resources, its similar dependence on price signals rather than dialogue, and its extensive reach.

The procedural state In the procedural state, individuals make contracts with each other, these contracts taking a form prescribed (or permitted) by either statute or case law. All resources are acquired by means of the contract, through either allocation or purchase. Resources may have high or low mobility, depending on the legal processes involved. Communication is solely through contract signals and judicial decision. Contract processes are highly formal; and relations are horizontal. There is in principle a high capacity for enforcement through legal process, and this capacity has extensive reach throughout the society. The contract differs from the market in its strong capacity for enforcement.

The corporate hierarchy In the corporate hierarchy, all resource questions are handled through the internal managerial structure of large firms, including hierarchical relations between firms at different stages of the production process. All resources are endogenous to this hierarchy, and are allocated within it by administrative decision. Resources have high mobility, because they are at the disposal of the central management. Communication is through both signals and dialogue as this management chooses, these processes being formal. Relations are by definition vertical. There is a high capacity for enforcement, because of the authority of management, but reach is limited to the hierarchy itself. This also implies limited reach. The hierarchy stands alone among the forms of governance in many respects, in particular the endogenous nature of its resources. Elements of it are very widespread, large Japanese and Korean enterprises coming closest to the pure form.

The essentially hybrid nature of governance

It is clear from such an inspection of true ideal types of these modes of governance that hardly any of them is likely to be fully autonomous, certainly not in dealing with economic relations of any complexity. Some display a rigidity of resource allocation that makes it difficult for them to respond to changing demand among consumers (the substantive state, association, community). These modes exist only alongside market governance. This happens either openly and willingly, or (as in state socialism) in the form of black markets. Within a capitalist society the market is only absent from a few institutions, such as friendship and love relationships, and the postwar welfare state.

Some modes of governance lack autonomous external enforcement capacity (networks, markets), and have to coopt other modes when they extend beyond a narrow range. The procedural state is the main mechanism that performs this role. What is called the free market economy is always a hybrid between the pure market and the procedural state, and extension of the scope of the market often involves extension of this aspect of the state too. For example, when the German government wanted to move to a more 'US type' stock market system it had to replace voluntarist self-regulation with more centralised, statutory regulation à l'américaine; more market implied more (procedural) state.[13] Ironically, this system is said to operate only for a small number of firms who are the 'very largest and most influential in Germany'—that is, firms which do not really suit the neo-classical model of the firm.[14] This draws our attention to the mix between market and corporate hierarchy in any functioning model. In fact, what passes in most discussion for the 'market economy' is always a compound of market, procedural state and corporate hierarchy. As we have seen, hierarchy differs considerably from market as a form of governance. The compound of these three elemental forms therefore provides a governance mix of considerable potential diversity.

Within this compound form, the other governance modes operate by interposing themselves between firms and the MHP (market/hierarchy/procedural state) amalgam. For example, a firm embedded in a community within a market economy (as, for example, in the case of a small family firm in an Italian industrial district) is not engaged in a subsistence economy, but reaches out through its community to a market. A substantive state within a capitalist economy changes the way in which firms subject to its interventions encounter the market, but it does not suppress markets, and has to be careful of the impact of its actions on market forces. It behaves quite differently from

108

a state in a non-market economy, as can be seen from a comparison of the French and Russian economies during the postwar period.

It is possible to formulate other compound types. MHP will always predominate, but minority or even trace components of other governance forms can still be important, even decisive, in making niche characteristics available to certain kinds of producer in specific national or regional economies. (Similarly, while H_2O is always by far the dominant constituent of any bottled water, it is different combinations of sodium, potassium and other trace elements that impart distinctive flavour and other properties that determine the market niches of particular brands.) For example, in some economies associations play a particularly important role, as (in diverse ways) in the German and Scandinavian cases. This has some important implications for the conduct of those economies. Alternatively, in the US case, we would have to take account of the role of high-tech military expenditure as an important example of the substantive state, rather small roles for associations and communities, but sometimes a larger one for networks. To give a more accurate account still, this would need to be nuanced according to sector and locality. For example, in sectors dominated by small firms hierarchy plays a smaller role relative to market; in sectors dominated by government contracts (aerospace, some aspects of computers and information technology) the substantive state is more important. In several high-tech sectors network plays a strong role, as already indicated above.

Finally, different modes of governance might prevail across different resource areas. It might be possible, for example, for an economy which has an industrial relations system dominated by corporatist (associational) structures to have vocational education located mainly in state institutions with little corporatist involvement (as in the case of Sweden).[15]

Markets and hierarchies

Relations between the market and the corporate hierarchy require some further discussion, as they are subject to considerable misunderstanding. During the 1990s it seemed that the firm as an institution, the heart of the corporate hierarchy mode, might be deconstructing itself into nothing other than a set of markets. Decision making power seemed to be passing from stable ownership groups and senior managers into the hands of constantly changing owners of shares, who related to the firm solely through market acquisition and sale of its assets. What had previously been interpreted as the power of management was seen to have become subordinated to the need to maximise shareholder value. Meanwhile, employment contracts were seen to be disappearing, as firms turned former employees into self-employed subcontractors and franchisees, with whom the firm had a purely market relationship. This account of an imminent deconstruction of the firm as organisation into a set of markets served a number of purposes. For neo-liberals it suggested that the theory of the firm and other forms of economic analysis outside the neo-classical frame were redundant; the market was the only institution in existence.

For Third Way writers, the incredible lightness of being of the new economy paralleled their general preference for 'light' institutions—as for example in Charles Leadbeater's concept of 'thin air'.[16] Also, the apparent disappearance of both management and the status of employee marked a final end to class relationships, and the replacement of the classic Old Labour figure of the employed worker by a society of entrepreneurs.

But these authors were extrapolating from a few cases, and distorting even the evidence of those. Share markets certainly did assume a new importance. The major waves of asset stripping that had accompanied the deindustrialisation of the 1980s had left large quantities of capital seeking investment opportunities. Meanwhile certain new developments, mainly in information technology, were creating such opportunities. However, most existing firms continued to rely primarily on internally generated funds rather than the markets for investment funds. Further, the move away from employment status was limited. Firms used it when they were uncertain about their future employment needs, and for marginal types of work. But for core tasks that were fundamental to the firm's own knowledge base, its public presentation and its corporate culture, they preferred to retain employees of the familiar type. There has been no general deconstruction of the corporation. In fact, globalisation has given a renewed prominence to vast multinationals—even in the new, post-Fordist sectors, as is demonstrated by the case of Microsoft. Meanwhile, Enron and a number of other scandals showed that corporate top managers could be very resourceful in evading the scrutiny of shareholders.

Even where disintegration of employment status and of the organisational shape of the corporation did take place, this did not represent a collapse of large concentrations of capital. Rather, management used the possibilities for organisational flexibility as a strategy, deciding whether to outsource or retain in-house a function depending on the firm's needs. When we see a corporate hierarchy extending to large numbers of dependent supplier companies and subcontractors we are seeing, not the end of the hierarchy and of the firm as organisation, but their complete expression.

Appreciation of the importance of corporate hierarchy and its relationship to markets is highly important to an evaluation of the frequent juxtaposition between the state and the market. The state's interactions with firms are more often than not with large corporations, which make use of the organisational resources of hierarchy as much as those of the market. This has a number of implications.

First, relations between the state and large corporate organisations have a different quality from relations within the market. In the pure neo-classical concept of the market, all transactions are anonymous, there are no enduring relations (other than series of repeated one-off transactions), and no one firm or individual is capable of setting a price or making a deal other than as

110

determined by market forces. Political lobbying by firms cannot even be conceptualised in such a context. This is why advocates of free markets reasonably claim that such a system is corruption proof and manipulation proof. But that is not the case with corporate hierarchies, which lack all these characteristics of markets. When governments announce that they are bringing in market forces, and set about this by negotiating closely with a small number of chosen firms, they are engaged in an oxymoron. They are bringing together, not state and market, but state and corporate hierarchy.

Second, the firm as organisation has many similarities to the state as organisation, which considerably reduces some of the contrasts drawn between states and markets in polemical debate. For example, it is often argued that private firms will have more regard for customers than public services, because the profits of the firms depend on satisfying customers. But the employees of, say, a large supermarket chain do not have this profit motive. Their position is the same as that of a public service employee: they have an employment contract, which gives them incentives to behave in certain ways. If the senior management of the supermarket chain want their employees to deliver good customer service, they manipulate their earnings and their training and supervision to give them incentives to do so. Similarly, if the political heads of a public service consider that their reputations will be affected by the quality of public services, they can require that their organisations provide very similar kinds of incentive. Large firms and governments share many characteristics, and they can and do learn from each other.

The state and complex governance

When we see the modern economy in terms of combinations of these various modes of governance, we are able to transcend the politicised dichotomy between state and market. These combinations can be used, not only at the level of analysis, but also in prescriptions for the future of the economic role of the state. During the high tide of the Keynesian and Fordist economy—broadly the third quarter of the twentieth century—there was a certain stability in economic governance. It did not comprise government alone, as some recent literature would have us see it, but a combination of at least state, market and corporate hierarchy; in some cases (such as the Nordic countries, Germany) associations were also important; in others (Italy, for example), community. Since the collapse of the Keynesian framework, there has been more experiment with governance forms. Networks have assumed an importance in several high-tech sectors. Governments have experimented with encouraging new combinations of links among networks, firms, local governments and markets. Privatisation and public subcontracting can also be analysed in this way, as shifts in the balance among the substantive state, corporate hierarchies and markets. Not many settled patterns emerge from this process, because the twenty-first century

economy has few stable predictable points. No one knows which combinations will bring results, and those that gave results at one point in time or
space may not do so in another.

Some particularly interesting experiments take place at the levels of cities
and regions.[17] This is so for two reasons. First, the low level of autonomy of
formal authorities at these levels makes them less jealous of sovereignty than
nation states. Second, the policy issues here are often to do with economic
development, where partnerships with firms, associations and networks can
be important. Sheffield provides an interesting example.[18] As a steel city, it
had been a classic case of Fordism. Economic governance was in the hands
of the corporate hierarchies of the great steel firms, which mainly worked
directly with central government. The city council took the city's economy
for granted. The collapse of the sector in the 1980s coincided with the high
tide of neo-liberalism. In what became famous as the 'People's Republic of
South Yorkshire', Sheffield city council, then of the far left, tried to run a
substantive state economic governance virtually alone. This was impossible;
the market was really the dominant force in the city's economy as the large
firms collapsed and withdrew. The local state was fighting the market, not
working in partnership with it. It had a concept of partnership, working
with networks and associations of business, but initially did not know how
to make the compromises necessary to make a hybrid form of governance
from this.

It gradually learned to do so. Faced with a hostile central state and a
collapsing economy, the council, and the networks, associations, and individual corporate hierarchies of the city's businesses realised that they formed
a community of fate and began to cooperate. The word 'Partnership' was used
in an almost talismanic way by all. One cannot yet say that Sheffield has
found an autonomous, post-steel economic future; the city depends too much
on call centres and decentralised back offices. But as a system of urban
governance it is more diverse and complex, joining all modes of governance
analysed here, except possibly community, than in either of its two earlier
manifestations.

Another interesting case is the media sector of the city of Cologne.[19] The
economy of this city has long been more diverse than that of Sheffield, and
there has been no crisis. However, the media sector (in particular film and
television) has come to play a particularly vibrant part in the urban economy.
It resembles Sheffield only in that this sector, like Sheffield steel, had been
dominated by a large organisation: one of the public broadcasting companies
had its headquarters there. Governance of the sector was therefore heavily
dominated by the simple model of the corporate hierarchy. This was
challenged by the growth of private television, some decline of the public
sector, and the growth of new media and techniques of programme and film
making that used lighter, more flexible work arrangements. At a simple level,
one could argue that corporate hierarchy was now diluted, and loosened up,
by the market.

But closer inspection reveals a more complex scene. First, there has been a good deal of public policy by the city and the *Land* governments to encourage further growth of the sector by providing facilities for media firms. But second, this is a sector that depends on considerable informal personal interaction among a relatively settled but also fluid population. In this it resembles many other areas with sectors that experiment with the production and use of high technology; and also resembles other fashion-conscious industries, like the Italian clothing and jewellery sectors. In these types of activity ideas travel fast; knowledge accumulates rapidly and then becomes redundant; individuals possess important skills, but they are often difficult to certify. People need to know each other and stay around long enough to know and be known. The massive, anonymous fluctuations of a pure market system would be disastrous for this. But the exchanges of ideas and personnel needed to be flexible and capable of change—qualities not easily found in the solid structures of states, corporate hierarchies, communities or even formal business associations. An economy of networks is valuable. Individuals are more locally grounded, and also far less anonymous, than in the pure market. The economic governance of the Cologne media sector is therefore a combination of markets, networks, the substantive state, and still present if declining corporate hierarchies. If any element of this mix were missing, the sector would be different.

Two examples do not prove anything, though many other instances of experiments and shifts and recombinations of economic governance could be given. But the cases do illustrate some general points: there are more components to such governance than just states and markets; for different tasks very diverse combinations may be effective. It is still too early to tell whether the flurry of activity currently to be observed all over the advanced world is a long-term characteristic of a post-Fordist, postmodern economy and society, or whether it will settle down into some major patterns. Many failed experiments will eventually be cleared away, reducing diversity. However, we already know enough to judge that there is often more than one way of tackling the issues involved, suggesting that at least some untidy variability may be enduring.

The implications of all this for the role of the state are complex. We must first remember the useful division between the substantive and procedural states, differing from each other but both equally capable of steering and intervening. The state does not withdraw from the scene; it remains (often, but not solely, in its local form) an active mode of governance, and can be a vital component of experiment. Its role changes in comparison with the postwar Fordist and Keynesian state, but it changes within a context of change in other modes of governance too. In dynamic sectors networks are growing in importance at least as much as markets. Whether there is 'more' or 'less' state in an economy where the financial sector requires a close and constantly adjusting regulatory regime is also a matter for debate.

Another conclusion is that the more diverse the repertoire of potential forms of governance that there is in a particular context, the more scope those involved will have to experiment and respond to change. This may well be a principal lesson of the southern Californian high-tech economy. There is a combination here of multiple governance modes: markets; the corporate hierarchies in several sectors; the very extensive and important networks already described; and the procedural and substantive state at several levels. This latter includes the military arm of the central state, which is not only a major source of contracts for the aerospace, computing and semiconductor industries, but was also the initial form of governance for the internet and therefore a fundamental aspect of information technology.

Conclusions

A major problem of the present period is that during the 1980s social democrats were slower than neo-liberals to recognise that the ensemble of the postwar economy was changing. We tried to cling to the Keynesian formula after it had passed its time. This was mainly because manual workers and trade unions continued to have their centre of gravity in large manu-facturing firms, and they have been central to social democratic concerns. As a result, the neo-liberal perspective achieved a hegemonic position in defining and interpreting the terms of the twenty-first century economy. Contempor-ary revisionist social democrats of the Third Way type have not found a language or means of reform other than that of mimicking its message that the market is all. Corporate hierarchies are defined away, as we saw above; the other modes of governance are either ignored, stigmatised (as in Le Grand's case, cited above), or assimilated to the market, from which they in fact differ in various ways. The rich and complex mixes of economic governance that are appearing, and which Third Way thinking seemed poised to comprehend, are appreciated only through this distorting glass.

Social democracy will only develop its own approach to the post-Fordist economy when it gains a more detailed and more accurate perspective on the diversity of governance modes. It needs to lose its inferiority complex over the state and recognise its possibilities as a creative actor. This is a role that includes but is not limited to market making, as sometimes pure market forces might destroy the fine tissue of other mechanisms. It needs therefore also to gain a perspective on market forces and to avoid reducing all springs of innovation to them. And it needs to distinguish markets from corporate hierarchies, so that it can appreciate their respective advantages and pitfalls. A social democracy that could achieve this kind of balanced appreciation in both its rhetoric and its detailed policy-making would soon leave neo-liberals behind as blinded by dogma and unable to appreciate the complex nature of economic reality.

Notes

1 J. Le Grand, 'Tales from the British National Health Service: competition, co-operation or control?', *Health Affairs*, 1999, no, 18, pp. 27–37; and *Motivation, Agency and Public Policy*, Oxford, Oxford University Press, 2003.

2 Harold Wilson, *The Governance of Britain*, London, Weidenfeld and Nicolson, 1976.

3 R. Leach and J. Percy-Smith, *Local Governance in Britain*, London, Palgrave, 2001, p. 5.

4 See, for similar but less naive accounts: J. Greenwood, R. Pyper and D. Wilson, *New Public Administration in Britain*, London, Routledge, 2002; and R. Rhodes, *Understanding Governance*, Buckingham, Open University Press, 1997.

5 A. Giddens, *The Third Way: The Renewal of Social Democracy*, Cambridge, Polity, 1998, p. 7.

6 Ibid., pp. 77, 79.

7 A. Gamble, *The Free Economy and the Strong State*, Basingstoke, Macmillan, 1988.

8 C. Crouch, *Commercialisation or Citizenship: Education Policy and the Future of Public Services*, London, Fabian Society, 2003.

9 This general approach was first developed by J. Campbell, J. R. Hollingsworth and C. Lindberg, *The Governance of the American Economy: The Role of Markets, Clans, Hierarchies and Associate Behavior*, Berlin, Wissenschaftszentrum Berlin, 1985, in a study of the US economy, and developed further in a comparative context by J. R. Hollingsworth, P. C. Schmitter and W. Streeck, eds, *Governing Capitalist Economies: Performance and Control of Economic Sectors*, Oxford, Oxford University Press, 1994. It has considerable similarities to what a group of French scholars had identified as *régulation* (R. Boyer and Y. Saillard, *Théorie de la régulation: l'état des savoirs*, Paris, La Découverte, 1995). The two perspectives were brought together in J. R. Hollingsworth and R. Boyer, eds, *Contemporary Capitalism: The Embeddedness of Institutions*, Cambridge, Cambridge University Press, 1997.

10 This distinction is well set out by F. Van Waarden in 'Market institutions as communicating vessels: Changes between economic coordination principles as a consequence of deregulation policies', in J. R. Hollingsworth, K. H. Müller and E. J. Hollingsworth, eds, *Advancing Socio-economics: An Institutionalist Perspective*, Lanham, MD.: Rowman & Littlefield, 2002, pp. 171–212.

11 K. Ohmae, *Triad Power: The Coming Shape of Global Competition*, New York, Free Press, 1985.

12 A. L. Saxenian, *Regional Advantage: Culture and Competition in Silicon Valley and Route 128*, Cambridge, MA, Harvard University Press, 1994; M. Kenney, ed., *Understanding Silicon Valley: The Anatomy of an Entrepreneurial Region*, Stanford, Stanford University Press, 2000.

13 R. Deeg, *Institutional Change and the Uses and Limits of Path Dependency: The Case of German Finance*, MPIfG Discussion Paper 01/6, Cologne, Max-Planck-Institut für Gesellschaftsforchung, 2001; S. Lütz, *From Managed to Market Capitalism? German Finance in Transition*, MPIfG Discussion Paper 00/2, Cologne, Max-Planck-Institut für Gesellschaftsforchung, 2000.

14 Deeg, *Institutional Change and the Uses and Limits of Path Dependency*, p. 35.

15 C. Crouch, D. Finegold and M. Sako, *Are Skills the Answer?* Oxford, Oxford University Press, 1999.

16 C. Leadbeater, *Living on Thin Air*, London, Viking, 1999.

17 C. Crouch, P. Le Galès, C. Trigilia and H. Voelzkow, *Local Production Systems in Europe: Rise or Demise*, Oxford, Oxford University Press, 2001, and *Changing Governance of Local Economies: Response of European Local Production Systems*, Oxford, Oxford University Press, 2004.
18 C. Crouch and M. S. Scott, 'Regeneration in Sheffield: from council dominance to partnership', in Crouch et al., *Changing Governance of Local Economies*.
19 U. Glassmann and H. Voelzkow, 'Recombining governance modes: the media sector in Cologne', in Crouch et al., *Changing Governance of Local Economies*.

New Localism, Progressive Politics and Democracy

GERRY STOKER

NEW LOCALISM can be characterised as a strategy aimed at devolving power and resources away from central control and towards front-line managers, local democratic structures and local consumers and communities, within an agreed framework of national minimum standards and policy priorities.[1] In this chapter I explore how a commitment to New Localism in the governance of England is justified, indeed rather overdue, and how it might be associated with new forms of democracy and new institutions of the local state.

The call for a shift in the approach to reform and future governance has become quite fashionable within progressive political circles inside and outside New Labour ministerial circles and beyond. The breadth, variety and thrust of the agenda are captured by Alan Milburn—who has since returned to government to lead on strategy—in a speech delivered in March 2004.[2] It is worth quoting at length the views of a relatively recent convert to localism:

> I believe we have reached the high water mark of the post-1997 centrally-driven target-based approach. That view is also widely shared in government. Reforms to enhance choice, diversify supply and devolve control are all now taking hold as the Government moves from a centralised command and control model to what has been called new localism. The issue now is how much further to go. . . . Public services cannot be run by diktat from the top down. In this next period, accountability needs to move downwards and outwards to consumers and communities. Empowering them is the best way to make change happen.

There are differences of emphasis among government ministers about how to take forward the New Localist agenda. The Blair camp is more willing to go along with user or consumer choice and the Brown camp is less keen but still interested in the issue of how public services can be 'personalised' and made more responsive to users. Sometimes the emphasis is on managerial reform, giving more power to head teachers or community based police commanders; on other occasions it is much more explicitly about giving communities or citizens control, wrapped up in a wider expansion of civil renewal as suggested in the speeches of David Blunkett. For some, established local government needs to be brought back into the frame as central to New Localism; others are not so convinced and have other institutions to steer local governance in mind.

There is undoubtedly much that is pure rhetoric in the new found interest on the part of New Labour in localism and much that represents a strategic political response to the possibility that the Conservatives might use localism to attack the control freakery, state paternalism and big spending plans that

© The Political Quarterly Publishing Co. Ltd. 2004
Published by Blackwell Publishing Ltd, 9600 Garsington Road, Oxford OX4 2DQ, UK and 350 Main Street, Malden, MA 02148, USA

could be said to characterise many of New Labour's policies. Yet in this essay I argue that the shift in thinking implied by the embrace of New Localism has some substance and value. In short, it represents a practical response to a significant practical challenge: how to manage a substantial variety of state service provision and interventions in a world that defies the application of simple rule-driven solutions and often requires an effective response from the recipient of the service or intervention in order for the state action to work.

The complexity of what the modern state is trying to achieve, the need for a more engaging form of politics and a recognition of the importance of issues of empathy and feelings of involvement to enable political mobilisation make the case for a New Localism because it is at the local level that some of these challenges can best be met. The point is not that all political action and decision should be local but rather that more of it should be. These arguments occupy the first section of the chapter.

The vision of New Localism needs to be carefully specified in a way that recognises diversity in communities and a concern with equity issues. The argument is not for a romantic return to community decision making or a rampant 'beggar my neighbour' localism. It is about a key and growing role for local involvement in decision making about the public services and the public realm as part of a wider system of multi-level governance. These clarifications and caveats about the nature of New Localism are dealt with in the second section of the chapter. The final section tries to put some flesh on the bones of the argument and explores the form of local state organisations that might express that New Localism in practice.

Justifying New Localism

The case for New Localism rests on three grounds. First, it is a realistic response to the complexity of modern governance. Second, it meets the need for a more engaging form of democracy appropriate to the twenty-first century. Third, New Localism enables the dimensions of trust, empathy and social capital to be fostered and as such encourages civic engagement. Each of these arguments will be explored further below.

Complexity

There are very few problems confronting communities today that have simple solutions. Protecting the environment, creating a sound economy, sustaining healthy communities or helping to prevent crime all require a complex set of actions from people and agencies at different spatial levels and from different sectors. It would be nice to argue that we should stop doing complexity and instead think about simplicity. That might wash in a self-improvement book but when it comes to running the business of a modern society the attraction of simplicity is false. As the saying goes, 'To every complex problem there is a simple answer and it is always wrong'.

We need to find ways of living with complexity. We need to understand any problem or an issue in its multiple dimensions and find mechanisms that enable us to not get swamped by complexity but to deal with it effectively. That is where the message of New Localism has got something to offer. The path to reform is not to allow local institutions complete autonomy or equally to imagine that the centre can steer the whole of the government system. We need a form of central–local relations that allows scope for all institutions to play an active role, and we need to find ways of involving a wider range of people in the oversight of the services that are provided through public funds and in the search for solutions to complex problems.

Complexity comes in a range of forms: structural, technical or over the allocation of responsibilities. Indeed, as Saward notes, 'one of the key challenges to democracy today lies precisely in the sheer complexity of modern government and governance'.[3]

Complexity is inevitable because of the range of activities that governments and public services are now engaged in. There are as a result a lot of organisations involved in delivery. There are the formal levels of government at Westminster, in the devolved parliaments, and in local authorities and parish and community councils, soon, perhaps, to be joined potentially by regional assemblies in specific parts of England. There are, in addition, organisations that make up a vast army of quangos, appointed boards and partnership bodies. As Sullivan and Skelcher argue, we live in a 'congested state'.[4]

Complexity also results from the sheer technical difficulty of what we now attempt to do in the public sphere. We have moved from hard-wiring challenges to a concern with soft-wiring society. It was enough of a challenge to build schools, roads and hospitals and ensure the supply of clean water, gas, electricity and all the requirements of modern life. Recent (late 2003) events in the USA and Canada with major power failures remind us that even hard wiring can still go wrong big time! But so much of what we are trying to do now is about soft wiring, getting healthier communities, ensuring that children from their early years get the right stimulation and the right environment in which to grow and develop, trying to find ways in which our economy can grow in a way that meets the challenges of globalisation and the need for sustainability. Soft wiring challenges are complex.

Complexity is also reflected in that there is a boundary problem in a lot of public policy arenas. Who is responsible for keeping us healthy? Is it the citizen who should eat and drink appropriately, the state that should provide good advice, or companies that should sell healthier food? We know it unfair to ask the police, on their own, to solve the problem of crime. We know that for our children to become educated needs more than better schools. In short, complexity comes from the fact that the boundaries between sectors of life and different institutions have become increasingly blurred.

So complexity of function, scale, purpose and responsibility are part of the modern condition. What does New Localism deliver in the light of complexity? New Localism is attractive because it is only by giving scope for local capacity building and the development of local solutions, in the context of a national framework, that we can hope to meet the challenge posed by these complexities. The solution to complexity is networked community governance because it is only through such an approach that local knowledge and action can be connected a wider network of support and learning. In that way we can get solutions designed for diverse and complex circumstances.

Networked community governance sets as its over-arching goal the meeting of community needs as defined by the community within the context of the demands of a complex system of multi-level governance.[5] The model demands a diverse set of relationships with 'higher' tier government, local organisations and stakeholders. The relationships are intertwined and the systems of accountability are multiple. The political process is about identifying problems, designing solutions and assessing their impact. Success is not a simple matter of efficient service delivery but rather the complex challenge of whether an outcome favourable to the community has been achieved. The responsibility ids not just to deliver certain services well but steer a community to meet the full range of its needs. The model takes up the challenge of holistic working which is achieving 'greater effectiveness in tackling the problems that the public most care about'.[6]

Democracy: engaging participants

To commit to New Localism means recognising that conventional understandings of democracy are valuable but limited. We can agree that several of the features of conventional visions of democracy remain essential: the protection of fundamental citizen rights and freedom of organisation and assembly for groups and individuals. But we need we need different answers to two fundamental questions: what are the building blocks of democracy, and what is the nature of accountability? The conventional answer to these two questions in the UK sees the nation-state, parliament and central government as the ultimate and indeed prime building blocks of democracy and accountability as led by elected representatives being held to account by their electorates. This top–down view of democracy is not appropriate when we think about making democracy work in our complex societies.

New Localism draws in broad terms from the ideas of associative democracy advocated by the late Paul Hirst, although it should be said straight away that our approach is a good deal more piecemeal and partial than the vision set out by Hirst. However, we take from his writings (in particular, 'Democracy and governance'[7]) four essential insights.

First, that democracy must have a strong local dimension; the core institution of democracy is not the nation-state. Democracy is made real through its practice at local, regional and international levels as well as at the level of the nation-state. More than that, central government should be an enabler, regulator and maybe a standard setter but not a direct provider nor the level for coming to judgements about detailed directions or the substance of services. Second, that provision itself must be plural through a variety of organisations and associations so that everyday citizens have an opportunity to be involved in decisions about services and judge the capacity of different institutions to deliver. Third, democracy can be organised through functional as well as territorial forms. Users of a particular service, those concerned with a particular policy issue, form as legitimate a political community as those that come from a particular territorial base. Finally, this understanding of democracy sees accountability as a more rounded process. The electorate choosing their representatives remains important, but people should have more opportunities to be involved in direct discussion with service providers and be in a position to judge their performance. In short, accountability involves reason-giving, questioning and a continuous exchange between the provider and the relevant public. The service providers will also have accountability to the centre in terms of the minimum standards. The lines of accountability are multiple and overlapping.

Building social capital

One key area where this new vision of democracy has the potential to deliver is with respect to the hidden social fabric of trust, social capital and citizenship that makes a key contribution to tackling the complex service and policy issues that we now face.[8] We need to find ways in which these resources among ordinary citizens can be fostered and replenished. A New Localist policy has the potential to be centrally important in developing these resources.

We know that involvement and exchange are the crucial ways in which trust and social capital are created and sustained. A democracy of strangers loses these dimensions, yet both trust and social capital are essential for encouraging the commitment and providing the glue that allows solutions to complex problems to be identified and followed through. Trust and the sense of shared values, norms and citizenship that is encouraged through social capital can make people willing to go the extra mile in the search for solutions; it can enable agreements and collective action. A local dimension to governance can draw particularly effectively on these social dimensions of decision making.

The essential insight of social capitalists is that the quality of social relations makes a difference to the achievement of effective outcomes when it comes to activities that involve complex exchange of ideas and the coordination of a variety of actors. To buy a loaf of bread requires little in the way of intensity of social relations, but to come to a judgement about the use of open space in a community or to take on the commitment for a project to clean up the local environment does require effective networks of information flow, trust and some shared norms. Local or community governance can deliver that capacity and help to meet challenges that top–down government simply lacks the strength of social relations to deliver.

Clarifying New Localism: avoiding romanticism and addressing equity concerns

Progressive politics has often expressed an uncertainty about the value of local decision making. There are two common grounds for objecting to local decision making. One line of argument is that the perspective of communities is inherently limited and limiting. The danger of local decision making is that it opens up too much decision making to the parochial concerns of narrow-minded individuals and threatens the ideas and practice of a wider progressive politics. Behind the romantic notions of community lurks a real world of insular, 'not in my own back yard' politics. Progressive politics requires a wider canvas than that the local politics can provide. The second objection is that if the problems faced by communities are going to be addressed there is a need for interventions to address the inequalities faced by particular communities. To tackle inequality requires national or even international intervention, and creating more scope for local decision making simply helps to foster or even reinforce existing inequalities. Rich areas will stay rich and poor areas will be allowed the freedom to spend non-existent resources on addressing the problems they confront.

It is precisely because of recognition of these concerns that 'new' is added to the localism advocated in this essay. New Localism is crucially set in the context of national framework setting and funding. Indeed, the localism that is advocated is part of a wider system of multi-level governance as noted before. Moreover, there is nothing in New Localism that means that it simply assumes that local politics is automatically devoid of the tensions that characterise politics at other levels. Conflict between interests and the resolution of those conflicts remain at the heart of politics wherever it is conducted. Localism does not imply a sort of romantic faith in communities to come up with solutions for the common good. Nor is it incompatible with a redistribution of resources provided through the power of higher levels of government.

The argument for New Localism is an argument, in England at least, for a shift in the balance of governance, one that allows more scope for local decision making and local communities. It is premised on the idea that involving people in the hard, rationing choices of politics in the context of a shared sense of citizenship is a way of delivering a more mature and sustainable democracy. It is also based on the idea that meeting the challenge of equity does not mean treating all communities or individuals the same but rather it involves tailoring solutions to meet particular needs. That proposition would be widely accepted, and localism can play a part in ensuring the tailoring process succeeds and is responsive to local needs and circumstances.

Reforming the local state: meeting the institutional needs of New Localism

New Localism needs to find institutional expression. In this section we explore some of the options in terms of the local state.[9] This is not to deny that there is a wider civic infrastructure of intermediate organisations that will need to be enhanced if people are to be re-engaged in local politics. The local media, local groups and other community organisations can play a key part in providing the motivation and support that people need if they are to engage effectively. But the formal organisation of local politics also makes a difference.

More directly elected single-purpose bodies

One institutional option would be to consider the idea of having more directly elected local bodies with a defined purpose to sit alongside an elected local council that as now would have a mixed range of purposes. Such a move might be justified for the oversight of police services, health care provision, the management of local parks and other services or community facilities. The government has proposals for elections to the boards of foundation hospitals and seems willing to consider further moves in that direction in the health field.[10] The Home Office has suggested the idea of direct election for local police authorities; Hazel Blears, a Home Office minister, takes the argument even further and suggests 'one possibility is that every adult voter in the geographical area served by a hospital or primary care trust, school, college, social service—or even parks and leisure facilities—should be given a vote to elect some or all of the non-executive directors as part of a stakeholder board'.[11] The arguments for such a development rest on a perceived need to give local people more control over local public provision, to enable people to participate outside of the boundaries of mainstream party politics and to open up the operation of public service to more mutual forms of ownership and involvement by local communities.

Some claim that the election of single purpose bodies would make joint working impossible.[12] I would counter that there are practical concerns that would have to be addressed but there is no reason in principle why directly electing single purpose bodies would lead to the balkanisation of local governance. Indeed, in bringing direct election into play some of the harder aspects of partnership may well be delivered.

First the enemy of joining up is not specialisation, but fragmentation.[13] Supporters of joining up should not think that everything should be lumped together in some sort of vast organisational amalgamation. Indeed, joining up starts from the premise that many players have different experiences and capacities and as such have something of value to bring to the table. The point is to get them to the table in a way that joint objectives can be pursued, and that allows collaboration to develop. Having separate bodies therefore is not an argument on its own to suggest that fragmented government will result.

There is no reason to insist that direct election will make cooperation harder. The assumption appears to be that competing mandates will render all joining up more problematic. But does this add up? How come Conservative controlled Kent appears quite able to construct deals with a Labour government? How is it that Liverpool's Liberal Democrat run council and Labour controlled Manchester are working together more than ever before? Electoral mandates can sharpen the objectives of different agencies but that does not mean that those objectives cannot be achieved in cooperation with others.

The achievements of partnership at the local level are considerable. But there are limits, especially when it comes to committing the budgets and policy priorities of partners. Reference back up to central government ministers for those agencies not currently locally accountable hardly ever delivers the flexibility and capacity to respond to local circumstances. As things are, partnerships dance to the tune of a new centralism in which partners are always looking back to the centre for funding and approval. Current partnerships are as a result much talk and occasionally action. To deliver more of the action requires a local decision making process that can divert the resources and priorities of the partner organisations. Direct election might deliver that capacity to local decisions and at the same time be seen as a gain for local democracy, given that most of the proposals for direct elections in health or the police service mean adding an elected element where one has been absent in the past.

If the number of elected local bodies was increased so that each of us was involved in dozens of local elections each year then the danger of voting fatigue would raise its head. There would be dangers in such a development because the absence of effective electoral challenge and involvement opens the way to producer capture or the domination by a particular interest or user group. Indeed, criticisms have been levied in the past against multipurpose local government on these grounds; low turnout or lack of interest from the majority of voters threatens the legitimacy of any elected body whether it is single purpose or multipurpose. One option would be to have a series of same day elections, combined with extensive postal voting, as the most likely way to support turnout in both multipurpose local authorities and single purpose agencies. That might be so, but there is probably a case for experimentation. Overall it would be a more sensible option to restrict direct election to those agencies and functions that have sufficient salience to attract a public debate and therefore will provide the infrastructure for a democratic choice to be made.

A stronger neighbourhood government

There is considerable interest in the idea that more decisions could be taken at a spatial scale closer to people's felt sense of identity. One problem with British local governance, so the argument goes, is that it has been reorganised in a way that gave a priority to the alleged efficiency gains of operating at a larger scale but in the process has lost touch with people's felt sense of community. Compared to other local government systems in other Western democracies, the size of local government in Britain in relation to the population it covers is large, at least four times as large as in most other Western democracies. If there was a move to a unitary local government system across the whole of Britain, something that will be delivered in those areas where elected regional assemblies are chosen as an option, then the institutional space might be opened for a move to neighbourhood governance on a scale and with a level of substantive decision making not previously seen in British local government. This shift is an option that is being actively considered both within government and outside.

One way forward would to start with a new institutional clean sweep and abolish all parish councils (that exist largely outside urban areas) and clear the decks of the various council run neighbourhood committees and central government sponsored neighbourhood projects. These neighbourhood arrangements would be replaced by a new style elected neighbourhood council available to all communities, with responsibility for a range of local services and functions (parks, public and open spaces, community facilities, local lighting schemes and other quality of life issues), and an ability to raise a modest local tax in order to at least part-fund its provision and activities.

Another option is to build on what exists and try to make it more comprehensive, coherent and extensive. The organisation of parish councils that operate in rural areas could be updated and similar organisations established in urban areas. The neighbourhood councils and management schemes sponsored by local and central government could be developed in order to give them a more permanent and effective institutional life. A number of councils are exploring ways in which non-executive councillors can again become engaged in making decisions for and with their local communities in area or neighbourhood committees of various sorts.

There would be a number of challenges to be met if area or neighbourhood government were to grow and make a difference. There are issues about whether the role of the neighbourhood decision making could be established in a manner sufficiently independent of the decisions of other bodies. Without that independence it may be difficult to attract the engagement of local people, but too much independence could mean that wider local and national issues are neglected or blocked through institutionalised nimbyism. For example, if national demands call for new housing development then a local governance system that gave a planning veto to local neighbourhoods could be viewed as economically dysfunctional. There would probably be tensions between local authority councillor representatives and community representatives and disputes over competing legitimacies. There may be issues over the training and skill development of such a large number of community decision makers. There may well be cost issues, given neighbourhood government implies some loss of economies of scale.

None of these issues causes fundamental damage to the argument for more neighbourhood government, but they do present challenges that would have to be met. What is particularly attractive about this option is that it provides a way of making local government local. Involvement in neighbourhood government for many people would not be a full time or near full time occupation as it is for many councillors, even after the 2000 Act. ELG research shows that in 2003 even non-executive councillors claim to spend on average 73 hours a month on council business; for executives the figure increases to 113 hours.[14] For many people such time commitment is out of the question. The aim should be to create neighbourhood government in a way that is not so time demanding as the current system appears to be.

New technology may also aid exchanges and discussions. In particular, the arrival of 'social software' can facilitate internet exchanges between closed groups of individuals, creating an infrastructure for a series of 'invisible villages' in which neighbourhood issues could be hammered out without recourse to a never-ending series of time consuming meetings. This is not to gainsay the need for face-to-face exchange; it is just to accept that there are different ways of having a debate, and if neighbourhood government is to attract a wide range of new players to the world of local governance it needs to offer time efficient forms of involvement.

The rise of strategic local government

The world of local governance would benefit from further institutional diversity, but there will remain a central role for elected local authorities as the over-arching ring holders in their communities. Local authorities have through various pieces of legislation the capacity to perform this basic community leadership role. In some localities I can see a case for new additional powers to be given to local councils leading to a special charter status for those authorities that have the capacity to operate as the major strategic organisations for their area.

The immediate membership of such a group of charter authorities is likely to include the group of core cities outside London. If you look at the achievements of Birmingham, Leeds and Manchester in regenerating their cities and developing a powerful new vision of their localities it is difficult to deny that they have a visibility and impact in their role as local government that puts them in a different class to some of the other representatives of local government. Similarly, some of the county councils such as Kent have a capacity and ambitious agenda that set them apart. Some of the London boroughs, including Westminster, Wandsworth, Camden, and Hammersmith and Fulham, have shown a considerable ability to innovate and lead change in their communities. These authorities would be among the leading candidates for charter status but there are other councils that could establish their case. The key point is that some local government operates on a scale and with a capacity and breadth of agenda that make it capable of offering powerful strategic local governance for an area, yet the current legislative framework gives no recognition to that difference.

The aim would be to give substantially greater fiscal and legislative powers to the charter authorities. They would have an ability to raise funds and a wider range of functions to take into their orbit. The innovation forum of authorities that achieved an excellent rating in the 2002 Comprehensive Performance Ratings have been considering a number of options that would provide them with quite radical new freedoms and flexibilities and it may be possible to extend the logic of some of what they are interested in to the position we are advocating, although in my model charter status reflects the capacity and significance of the authority rather than simply its achievement against a benchmark of management measures.

One idea that has been floated by a number of authorities is that they should not only take responsibility for existing local government functions but also be given oversight and direction with respect to employment and skills programmes, regeneration, police and even health in their area. The existing agencies dealing with these issues in their area should be subject to policy direction from a group of elected councillors chosen to serve the local authority and subject to overview and scrutiny from a group of councillors chosen to serve the local authority. For example, a Hammersmith and Fulham council could be elected and then executive councillors chosen from within its midst could oversee not only the local authority core business but a range of the functions covered by some of the agencies in its area. The remaining councillors would become the scrutinisers of the performance of these agencies as well as the core local authority. As for funding, these councils would benefit from both control over blocks of funding provided for the agencies they are overseeing and potentially new revenue raising options: perhaps a marginal local income tax, a tourist tax, a share of any increase in business rate they generate. One other option is that if a policy initiative saved money then the savings could be inherited by the local authority to be used for other purposes. For example, Kent County Council has proposed that if it was able to get more local people into work in its area then some of the savings in the social security budget could go to the County Council and its residents.

There are a number of difficulties in the way of establishing strategic local government. The process by which councils were chosen for the freedoms and flexibilities associated with charter status would have to be open, transparent and fair, and not a matter of political favouritism. I accept that there would have to be some minimum threshold of performance that a council would have to pass in order to get charter status. The rule could be that no council that could only reach poor or weak standard in its quality of management and service delivery (as in the comprehensive performance assessment process or a similar successor) should be allowed to obtain or retain charter status. The basic principles behind the idea of charter authorities build on what, in part, made local government great in the nineteenth century. Local government status and functions allocated to local decision makers reflected the capacity of local decision making. When there was a capacity to take local control, then a request was presented for city or borough status along with the powers associated with that status. So one option in the current circumstances would be that where cities, towns or counties are able to demonstrate that they have the vision and wherewithal to deliver that vision then they should be given the freedoms and support necessary to sustain their efforts.

New Localism means shifting the pattern of governance in Britain and creating a more differentiated local state system that is suited to involving a wider range of participants as governors and adaptable to the different circumstances of various communities. It should be a central plank of progressive politics for the next quarter of a century. Given the previous quarter of a century of unrelenting centralism it is going to take that long to redress the balance; it will be a long time before we have to ask if localism has gone too far.

Notes

1 D. Corry and G. Stoker, *New Localism: Refashioning the Centre–Local Relationship*, London, New Local Government Network, 2002; D. Corry, W. Hatter, I. Parker, A. Randle and G. Stoker, *Joining-Up Local Democracy: Governance Systems for New Localism*, London, New Local Government Network, 2004.
2 A. Milburn, 'Active citizenship: the ten year agenda', speech to the Community Consultation Conference, London, 2 March 2004.
3 M. Saward, *Democracy*, Cambridge, Polity, 2003, p. 98.
4 H. Sullivan and C. Skelcher, *Working across Boundaries*, Basingstoke, Palgrave, 2002.
5 G. Stoker, *Transforming Local Governance*, Basingstoke, Palgrave Macmillan, 2004.
6 Perri 6, D. Leat, K. Seltzer and G. Stoker, *Towards Holistic Governance*, Basingstoke, Palgrave, 2002, p. 46.
7 P. Hirst, 'Democracy and governance', in J. Pierre, ed., *Debating Governance*, Oxford, Oxford University Press, 2000.
8 R. Putnam, *Bowling Alone: The Collapse and Revival of North American Community*, New York, Simon and Schuster, 2000.
9 See also G. Stoker and D. Wilson, eds, *British Local Government into the 21st Century*, Basingstoke, Palgrave Macmillan, 2004.
10 J. Reid, *Localising the National Health Service*, London, New Local Government Network, 2003.

11 H. Blears, *Communities in Control: Public Services and Local Socialism*, London, Fabian Society, 2003, p.18.
12 A. Pike, *The Disintegration of Local Government: Dangers of Single-service Elected Bodies*, London, Association of London Government, 2003.
13 Perri 6 et al., *Towards Holistic Governance*.
14 See www.elgnce.org.uk

Back to the Centre? Rebuilding the State

B. GUY PETERS

SINCE at least the early 1980s politicians, and even average citizens, have expended a great deal of time and energy dismantling the elaborate system of governing that had been built up during the preceding decades. The changes in the public sector went well beyond the 'liposuction' of eliminating substantial amounts of public expenditure during the 1990s. Political leaders in numerous countries have continued to implement reform programmes involving decentralisation, 'agentification', privatisation and deregulation, all changes intended to reduce the role of the public sector in the economic and social lives of their countries, and to move the governing activities that remain to the lowest possible level of government. The average citizen has played his or her role in this process of breaking down the governance system by expressing a rapidly declining confidence in the public sector,[1] by participating less in politics,[2] and (when participating) by voting frequently for politicians who pledge even further reductions in the role of government.

Even we lowly political scientists have played some minor role in this decline of the hierarchical state. From a variety of ideological perspectives scholars have advanced arguments to justify the continuing decline of the state, and especially of the capitalist welfare state, that had so recently had appeared to be such a great success.[3] In addition, some aspects of the growing body of literature on 'governance' have emphasised the weaknesses of hierarchical control within the public sector, and the capacity of self-organisation and networks to provide governance for societies on a more disaggregated, and potentially more democratic, basis.[4] The seeming impossibility of 'governance without government' has been advanced as a real possibility by some notable scholars in the discipline.[5]

Having created a highly disaggregated and decentralised apparatus to pursue public purposes, many political systems now face the perceived need to come full circle and to rebuild the state, or at least to rebuild some central governance capacity within the state. Concerns about the capacity to govern are hardly new. Elected political leaders have long expressed their discontent with their ability to govern, once elected. The power of entrenched political interests, and especially an entrenched public bureaucracy, often have been cited as barriers to elected leaders to govern and to implement the programmes that were contained in their platforms during the election campaign.

There are two important differences between some of the problems in governance in the early twenty-first century and those problems of the past.

 Published by Blackwell Publishing Ltd, 9600 Garsington Road, Oxford OX4 2DQ, UK and 350 Main Street, Malden, MA 02148, USA

The first difference is that many of the contemporary difficulties for political leaders have been designed into the reformed system of governing rather than represent the failure of the political apparatus to perform as designed, or rather to perform as assumed by the elected officials. Perhaps a better way of understanding these changes is that the reforms have been based on a theory of governing very different to that which had previously been dominant. This more contemporary notion of governing places much greater responsibility for the outcomes of the policy process on public sector managers, assuming that these individuals will have not only the technical ability to implement policy (rowing) but also the vision to guide policy (steering). Further, the contemporary model of governing is premised on the virtues of (relatively) autonomous organisations acting on their own to maximise their own efficiency and effectiveness. The summation of the efforts of these individual organisations and their leaders is assumed to constitute good government.

The second, and closely related, issue is that the governance problems characteristic of the contemporary period are appearing at the very centre of government, and face prime ministers and presidents as much as or more than they challenge individual functional ministers. The chief executive officers in government now confront the need of making that government work as something approximating a coherent whole. The political and media focus on presidents and prime ministers in much of contemporary governance makes it all the more important for these central executives to be able to create some level of coherence and coordination in the choice and implementation of policies. Arguably, those needs are more relevant now than they have been at any time since the Great Depression and the Second World War, but the capacity to create the coherence has been designed out of government.

Problems of governing in the decentred public sector

One means of capturing the range of changes that have occurred in the public sector since the time that Reagan, Thatcher and Mulroney[6] held office is to argue that the state has become 'decentred', and that the centre of government no longer has the control over policy that it once enjoyed, or at least was supposed to enjoy. Functions that had been components of the central government apparatus have been moved out of ministries or departments to autonomous and semi-autonomous organisations, usually referred to as 'agencies'.[7] The leadership of these organisations have been granted substantially greater autonomy for action than had been true of elements of ministries, and are subject to less direct control by political leaders than under previous managerial arrangements. At even more of an extreme economic activities have been privatised, and many social and educational activities increasingly have been delivered through complex arrangements with 'social partners' in the private sector. Likewise, activities in other policy sectors have been moved out of central control to subnational government, with central government perhaps maintaining a monitoring function, or perhaps ridding itself of the activities entirely.

Other characterisations of changes in the contemporary state such as 'the hollowing of the state' have been more general, and have included a variety of losses of governance capacity.[8] For example, in addition to the types of changes discussed in this chapter contemporary states are also argued to be losing governing capacity upwards to the international system. This loss of capacity is to some extent generalised, as in the arguments about the effects of globalisation.[9] Also, for the soon-to-be 25 countries of the European Union there is an even more extreme transfer of governing capacity, albeit one that has been conducted with the active involvement of the member states. Although these other losses of governance capacity are important, in this discussion I will be most concerned with the loss of control by actors at the very centre of government—presidents, prime ministers, ministers of finance and other political leaders who might be expected to play a key role in shaping policy.

The decentring of governing involves a very particular set of institutional and behavioural changes, but it has a wide range of effects on governing. Some of the changes involved are political, related to the capacity of those chief executives to provide the leadership to the public sector that is expected of those officials. Other aspects of the change are more administrative, and are related to the capacity of those officials to connect to the implementation structures that nominally serve them. Both of these kinds of change add up to a loss of governing capacity.

Accountability

The decentring changes described above mean first that political leaders have lost the capacity to control the delivery of many of the policies for which they are nominally responsible, and in some cases also have lost the power to formulate policy. Therefore, these political leaders are in the awkward position of retaining nominal responsibility for policies over which they have lost most practical control.[10] This loss by ministers and prime ministers of numerous levers of control over policies again must be understood as a product of conscious design of governance arrangement. These design elements in contemporary government make outrage and the political disparagement of bureaucrats—common reactions to failures of the policy-making system to respond to political direction—less meaningful as responses to the loss of influence over policy. Further, attempting to explain to the media and to the public that policy failures are beyond the control of the minister is likely to appear to an increasingly sceptical population to be passing the buck.

In addition to the frustration these changes may produce for political leaders, another casualty from decentring the state is effective accountability. Accountability must always be a central consideration in the management of any democratic political system, and perhaps all the more important when greater emphasis is placed on the role of public managers in making and delivering policies. The traditional model of accountability in parliamentary systems is one that holds ministers politically accountable for the activities of the organisations under their nominal supervision.[11] This model relies primarily on members of parliament to expose malfeasance and non-feasance by administrative actors.

In the managerialist thinking that has been a driving force for the decentring reforms already described, accountability of this vertical, political variety is much less important than in conventional models of governing. Although some substitutes for traditional accountability have been created—such as performance standards and accountabilities to stakeholders within each policy area—that crucial democratic connection between the public and their servants has been weakened. The structure of accountability that is being developed in some policy areas tends to limit the capacity of the public in general to influence the outcomes of the process at the same time as it empowers groups directly concerned with the issue. In this case, public engagement may not so much equate with accountability as with capture by those interests.[12]

Coordination and coherence

A second crucial problem in the decentred state is the increasing threat to coherence and coordination in government. The ministerial structure and specialisation that have been characteristic of the organisations of the public sector have always made coordination in government difficult to the extent that it is one of the longest running problems in public administration. The decentring reforms have, however, exacerbated those coordination problems and brought them to the centre of the political agenda in some political systems. Again, this difficulty largely has been designed into the reformed system of governing, rather than being the consequence of individual shirking or sabotage.[13] The greater autonomy granted to agencies and to other quasi-autonomous organisations has tended to laud their absence of coordination, rather than to assume that it constituted a problem for governing. Again, the underlying assumption has been that the individual actions of more or less autonomous organisations could be aggregated into good government.

Other aspects of the reformed state have contributed to the difficulties in creating coherence. Performance management was mentioned above as helping to correct the difficulties of accountability, but it may also make autonomous organisations more conscious of pursuing their own goals rather than any collective goals. Expending any resources on helping other organisations or on pursuing coordination may detract from achieving the performance goals on which the organisation is being judged. In this case, the conflict between the pursuit of organisational goals and collective goals in government is very clearly defined. There may be means of defining performance indicators for government as a whole, or for sectors of action (see below), but the basic impact of performance management systems is to separate rather than unite the components of the state.

The coordination and coherence problems are further exacerbated by the involvement of social partners and other stakeholders in the making and implementation of policy. Managers and politicians themselves must now play a 'two level game' when constructing policies, and negotiate intensively both with interests in society as well as with other parts of government. If the negotiations involve multiple and potentially competing interests, as they often do, then, having reached such an agreement with those actors, moving away from it for government-wide goals may be difficult. While these patterns of policy-making are not entirely novel, and also have numerous positive features for governing, their diffusion and increased legitimacy simply add to these burdens of coordination.

Relative losses

The powers of the centre of government are also relative to the governance challenges they face, and those challenges, as noted above, appear more significant in the current period than in much of the recent past. For example, countries within the European Union must be capable of speaking with a common voice when they go to Brussels.[14] This demand for a common voice is important for the current members of the Union, but is perhaps especially important for the countries that are candidate members that must negotiate for the best deal with the Union. Even for countries outside the European Union, membership in international organisations, and even participation in the international market, requires integration of the perspectives across government.

Although I have been focusing on the international dimensions of the governance challenge, there is a need to provide integrated leadership even in domestic politics and policy-making. One element of the negative reaction of citizens to their governments is the incoherence and apparent ineffectiveness of their governments. Citizens see that many activities of the public sector may be redundant and wasteful, and that at the same time there may be holes in social safety nets and other collections of programmes that should work together more effectively.

Responses to decentring

As I implied at the beginning of this chapter, political leaders in the centre of government have become somewhat discontented with their loss of capacity to steer and are making some concerted attempts to re-establish at least a portion of their role as the source of political ideas and initiatives. This reassertion of the primacy of politics[15] is by no means universal, and some political systems continue to revel in their decentralisation, or even to decentre the system further. Still, an increasing number of individual leaders and administrative systems are attempting to find ways of governing more effectively from the centre.

I should be quick to point out that the responses to decentring are by no means attempts to recreate the hierarchical state that had been developed to manage the mixed-economy welfare state of the postwar period. Any governance system redesigned to cope with the problems created by the decentring of the state will have to take into account some fundamental changes in the climate of ideas surrounding governing. While governments may make significant attempts to balance the autonomy created through the earlier reform process, and to design mechanisms for generating coherence, the influence of managerialist ideas and a widespread anti-government ideology are not being replaced entirely.

One of the more interesting examples of an attempt to recapture the primacy of politics can be found in Sweden. Sweden was the origin of the agency model that has been adopted by the United Kingdom and numerous other countries. Historically, the autonomy of the agencies in Sweden did not present much of a problem of control for the ministries and the cabinet, given the broad agreement on the goals of the social democratic welfare state. As the managerialist ideologies have strengthened the capacity for autonomy for the agencies, and consensus on policy has waned, government has sought to establish greater direct control. One possibility raised by a Royal Commission has been to reorganise the state significantly, reduce the autonomy of the agencies (or perhaps move them into the ministries), and ensure more direct political control over implementation.[16]

Some of the reactions to the loss of control in the centre of government would be considered retrograde, most notably increasing levels of politicisation in the civil service. Evidence from a number of countries in Western Europe and North America is that political leaders have sought to re-establish their control through increasing levels of political appointment in public administration.[17] For example, in New Zealand, which had introduced one of the more radical versions of decentring the state, there has been some substantial reassertion of the role of politics in shaping the state and its policies. Certainly, the state in New Zealand as it exists in 2004 is markedly different from that which preceded the 'revolution' in the public sector during the 1980s.

Some other responses to decentring government have been simply to return to the *status quo ante*, and to restore some of the mechanisms that have been dismantled. One example of this response has been the British government in essence taking back management of some aspects of the rail system from the private sector after privatisation became associated with numerous problems, most serious being several fatal accidents. Likewise, the Dutch experiment with ZBOs, with extremely high levels of autonomy, has been terminated and those organisations brought back to substantially greater control by elected politicians.[18] These are returns to the organisational and governance formats used in the past, but again this is being done in the context of models of governing that have been changed significantly.

The more important changes in governments have been to create innovative approaches to the challenges placed before them. In many ways these responses to the loss of influence from the centre have had the paradoxical result of decentred government resulting in approaches to governing that may become ever more centralised, and the control of those central actors in government may be increased. There is an unplanned process through which the powers of presidents and prime ministers, or at least their apparent position in governing, are increasing. This informal process depends in part upon the dominant position of these actors in the media, and also the importance of international affairs even for the outcomes of domestic issues. At the same time that this more informal change is occurring, however, there are also changes in governments that are designed to enhance the control of those central actors.

One of the best examples of that 'recentring' of government can be found in the experience of the Finnish government. After Finland joined the European Union the government found that it had difficulties in responding successfully to the demands of participation in the Brussels arena. Although the governance problems were highlighted by membership in the EU, some of the same difficulties were evident in coping with domestic policy issues. The semi-presidential structure of Finnish government, and a long history of a strong, if not dominant, public bureaucracy, was making central leadership difficult.[19] In a series of institutional innovations the Finnish government developed a means of identifying and then implementing priorities that cut across conventional ministerial responsibilities.

These mechanisms for enhancing coherence in the Finnish government are at once both political and administrative. On the one hand, the identification of the priorities for government is very political, being a task for each new government to undertake in the first weeks of its mandate. On the other hand, once identified by government, the implementation of the government programme involves senior public servants and the creation of an implementation structure that may involve numerous ministries and departments. All the relevant priorities cut across conventional structures of government and require budgeting and implementation mechanisms that are not tied to those structures. Throughout that process, however, the primacy of politics continues to be respected for the programme.

As political leaders have found themselves being faced with the challenges of coping with the international and European environments, they often perceived the need to be able to react in a more strategic and coordinated manner than in the past. Operating in the European Union, for example, has required governments to speak with a common voice in several different forums simultaneously, and to stress national priorities in those settings. The decentred manner of governing, however, would prevent governments from being able to present such a unified approach in Brussels or in the World Trade Organization, for example.[20]

Even in the absence of the necessity of participating effectively in the European Union, greater coordination and coherence are important for any government, and for a variety of reasons. The apparent confusion and incompetence that may result from the 'decentring' discussed above is one of several sources of the decline of public confidence in the public sector. Further, the absence of coherence and coordination makes government more expensive and less effective in achieving its policy goals. Finally, attempts by politicians to explain that 'it's nothing to do with me' are not likely to be well received by a sceptical population.

As presidents and prime ministers have found that they were responsible for steering the society in a more integrated manner but did not have the levers at hand to do so, they have begun to reshape their own offices and are attempting to develop an institutionalised capacity to steer and control government. To some extent this strengthening of the centre reflects political trends that have been noted as occurring for other reasons. The political focus on prime ministers has resulted at least in part from the influence of the media, and from the central positions of events such as European Summits and G7 meetings. Again, however, even these officials may find themselves with a great deal of publicity but without the controls over policy that they might expect to have.

Finally, there are changes in the ideas about governing that are important for explaining the attempts to cope with the decentred government. This development of ideas has been evident in attempts of the British government to create a 'joined up' government and a more integrated approach to the tasks of governing.[21] The idea of a joined up government has been used to restate the familiar need for coordination in a new and potentially more persuasive manner. Similar ideas about a joined up government have been adopted in Australia, and more recently there has been an attempt to create a 'whole of government' approach to the policy problems there.[22] Likewise, Canadian government institutions have stressed the need for horizontal government and a greater capacity to work across government.[23] In all of these cases the guiding assumption of the reformers in the public sector has been that the structure of government has become excessively specialised and the 'stovepipes' that are likely to arise in any government have become too strong.

These ideas about the need to manage in a more integrated or 'horizontal' manner are hardly broad, ideological statements about governing, but they have been used to justify and guide processes of changing institutions and patterns of governing. In the case of Britain, albeit less clearly than that of Finland mentioned above, one can also see the development of institutions designed to create the capacity for central control and policy management. The Cabinet Office has been enhancing its capacity for strategic planning and policy direction at the centre of government, and has sought to identify the principal priorities for government. Once those priorities have been established, they are implemented through more conventional means than those used in the Finnish example.

In addition to these more economically developed political systems such as Finland and the United Kingdom, the candidate countries for the European Union coming from Eastern and Central Europe also are facing severe challenges of being able to bargain with the Union and to create sufficient domestic governance capacity to be able to administer the *acquis* when (or if, in some cases) they are admitted. In these cases, after some time of almost populist democracy following their release from the rule of the Soviet Union these countries now face the need to steer more from the centre and to govern effectively. This is yet another version of recentring, one that is to some extent threatened by the popularity of New Public Management ideas in parts of the donor community.

As governments attempt to recentre their style of governing, however, they confront new challenges and dilemmas. The most important of these is that while strengthening the centre may overcome some of the problems that have been created by adoption of the decentralising ideas of NPM, there is the danger of going back to the old centralised, hierarchical system that was the cause of much of the recent innovation in governing. That traditional system has largely been delegitimated, but there is as yet little intellectual rationale for the return to a seemingly more centralised system of governing.

In addition to the absence of any clear principles to legitimate the attempts to impose a more centralised vision on governance, the other problem that governments may confront is that the initial round of reforms had produced numerous benefits. Given those benefits, institutional designers in the public sector must consider a means of providing greater coherence within the system while maintaining some of the efficiency and effectiveness benefits. Those benefits may not be widely recognised by the public, but there is reasonable evidence that governments are indeed performing individual service functions better—while paradoxically the system as a whole may not be.

Conclusion

My purpose in this article has not been to enumerate and describe a variety of institutional responses to the problems of governing, although that descriptive exercise can say a good deal about what is happening in the centre of government. Rather, the purpose is to emphasise the necessity of governance, even when many political actors and groups assume that effective governance can be achieved through extremely decentralised formats. While at one time hierarchy was the default option in government, now markets, or perhaps networks, are the assumed first choices for addressing public problems.

Although the default options for achieving the goals of governing have changed, the fundamental requirements have not. The central requirement is the capacity to establish, implement and monitor priorities for the public sector. The decentralised, 'decentred' form of governing that has become common in industrialised democracies, as well as in many other parts of the world, simply is not very good at performing those basic tasks. In particular, the decentralised form of governing is generally not capable of providing coherent and coordinated governance, and likewise is not good at deciding on broad priorities for the society. These requirements for effective governance are by no means guaranteed by the recentring of the state, but these changes may assist in rebuilding that capacity.

Notes

1 See, for example, Joseph S. Nye, Philip D. Zelikow and D. C. King, *Why People Don't Trust Government*, Cambridge, MA, Harvard University Press, 1997.

2 Paul Whiteley, 'The state of participation in Britain', *Parliamentary Affairs*, vol. 56, 2003, pp. 610–16.

3 Claus Offe, *Contradictions of the Welfare State*, London, Hutchinson, 1984.

4 Jan Kooiman, *Socio-Political Governance*, London, Sage, 1993; E. Sorenson and J. Torfing, 'Network politics, political capital, and democracy', *International Journal of Public Administration*, vol. 26, 2003, pp. 609–34.

5 R. A. W. Rhodes, 'The new governance: governing without governance', *Political Studies*, vol. 44, 1996, pp. 652–67.

6 See Donald J. Savoie, *Reagan, Thatcher, Mulroney: Search for the New Bureaucracy*, Pittsburgh, University of Pittsburgh Press, 1994.

7 Christopher Pollitt and Colin Talbot, *Unbundled Government*, London, Routledge, 2003.

8 See Patrick Weller, Herman Bakvis and R. A. W. Rhodes, *The Hollow Crown: Countervailing Trends in Core Executives*, New York, St Martin's Press, 1997.

9 Susan Strange, *Mad Money: When Markets Outgrow Governments*, Manchester, Manchester University Press, 1998.

10 See B. Guy Peters and Jon Pierre, eds, *Politicians, Bureaucrats and Administrative Reform*, London, Routledge, 2001.

11 P. Day and Rudolf Klein, *Accountabilities*, London, Tavistock, 1987.

12 Eva Sorenson and Jacob Torfing, 'Network politics, political capital, and democracy', *International Journal of Public Administration*, vol. 26, 2003, pp. 609–34.

13 John Brehm and Scott Gates, *Working, Shirking and Sabotage*, Ann Arbor, University of Michigan Press, 2000.

14 H. Kassim, A. Menon, B. G. Peters and V. Wright, *Coordination in the European Union: The National Dimension*, Oxford, Oxford University Press, 2000.

15 See G. Bouckaert, D. Ormond and B. G. Peters, *A Possible Governance Agenda for Finland*, Helsinki, Ministry of Finance, 2001.

16 SOU, *Utvecklingskraft for Hallbar Valfard* (Development for Sustainable Welfare), SOU 2003, p. 13.

17 B. Guy Peters and Jon Pierre, *The Quest for Control: Politicization of the Civil Service*, London, Routledge, 2004.

18 Sandra Van Thiel, *Quangocratization: Trends, Causes, Consequences*, Utrecht, University of Utrecht, 2000.
19 Geert Bouckaert, Derry Ormond and B. Guy Peters, *A Possible Governance Agenda for Finland*, Helsinki, Ministry of Finance, 2000.
20 See Kassim et al., *Policy Coordination in the European Union: The National Dimension*.
21 Perri 6, D. Leat, K. Seltzer and G. Stoker, *Towards Holistic Governance: The New Reform Agenda*, Basingstoke, Macmillan, 2002.
22 Australian Institute of Public Administration, *Working Together*, Canberra, AIPA, March 2002.
23 Herman Bakvis and Luc Juliet, *Horizontal Management in Canadian Government*, Ottawa, Canadian Centre for Management Development, November 2003.

Reclaiming 'The Public' through the People

HILARY WAINWRIGHT

KEYNES had a prescription for social analysis when change is in the air but not yet institutionally grounded—we should 'make a candid examination of our own inner feelings in relation to the outside facts'.

Attempting such an examination in regard to the public sector raises various questions. Has the last twenty year long wave of neo-liberalism immersed the institutions of social democracy irreversibly—such that they are now sunken ruins, excavatable only by the historian equivalents of deep sea divers—or could they be retrieved and updated? With deft, strategic digging, could the land yet be drained and reclaimed? And are there the resources, energy, people or shared intellectual vision for such a task?

Evidence that the powers of the state have not been submerged beyond reach was paradoxically supplied when the President of the United States—the least interventionist state in the Western world—and the Prime Minister of the UK—the state most aspiring to cut back its interventions in the market—were able, after September 11, to massively increase public spending on the military, and to control financial markets to block financial support for terrorists. Whatever the wider context of these acts, it is impressive that they were *possible*. Under different, more democratically accountable, politicians and institutions, could not such powers be used for peaceful purposes? How do we make state institutions, as they have been in the past, more effective instruments of social justice? What are the limits of this process?

Observing the consequences of, on the one hand, increased state involvement (until the reign of Margaret Thatcher) in British society and, on the other hand, efforts to reinstate the rule of the market, it seems what we need now is not a new 'brand' of mixed economy ('a third way'), nor a return to the pre-neo-liberal balance of the 1960's, but a 'third dimension'—one concerned with the principles of organisation internal to specific market and state institutions and of the relations between them. A three- rather than two-dimensional model of state versus market might open our minds to a variety of principles of organisation of state institutions and services, as well as market enterprises. The question becomes not 'More state or less state?', or 'More powerful markets or less powerful markets?' but 'What kind of state institutions or private enterprises? To meet what goals? Organised on what principles? With what kinds of organisation and management?'

Such questions will never flow from 'state-versus-market' thinking. But 'third dimension' questions are crucial and proliferating. *How* should state institutions be administered? *How* may democracy be deepened beyond its

© The Political Quarterly Publishing Co. Ltd. 2004

Published by Blackwell Publishing Ltd, 9600 Garsington Road, Oxford OX4 2DQ, UK and 350 Main Street, Malden, MA 02148, USA 141 electoral form, now proving so weak? *How* may public resources be managed responsively to the people who voted for them? And, within the market: *How* may enterprises be socially accountable, particularly when financial markets have effectively lifted off from the real economy, let alone the realities of society?

I shall argue here that the flaws we observe in the social democratic state, namely unresponsiveness to people's changing demands, and waste and corruption (though probably less than in the private sector), are not best remedied via the market but by democratic innovations in the organisation of the state, including the nature of public administration within state institutions—for instance, putting to more socially effective use the capacities of front line workers and skilled managers, and even using practical knowledge held by the *users* of these services. Similarly, I shall argue that the social irresponsibility of the private corporation cannot be overcome simply by state regulation. Nor is state ownership often a realistic or straightforward option. What is necessary is a fundamental transformation of the forces which drive investment—away from profit maximisation towards recognition of environmental, labour and other social concerns. This means deploying every possible lever for democratic accountability and social responsibility. One possibility is new institutions of democratic control over the pension funds which dominate the stock market.[1] Another is democratic deployment of state purchasing powers for social ends.

This third dimension of how institutions, public and private, are organised influences relations between the market and state. If public institutions are managed in a way which gives people a sense of genuine democratic control over them, then popular support for extending social control over private corporations is more likely. The more politicians encourage people to give up on state institutions, defaulting to a belief in private business as more 'natural', the more any socially radical transformation of market institutions will also fail to inspire the public support that it needs. For example, the mutualism of most building societies ended at a time when virtually no mainstream politician would stand up for democratic collective decision making. This becomes a vicious spiral downwards—democratic innovation in independent enterprises or voluntary associations is a seed bed for change in the organisation of the state.

Two models of 'state-versus-market' underpinned mainstream debates about public services in the 1980s and most of the 1990s. On the one hand, administered by professionals who 'knew' what people needed, there was the 1945 model of cradle to grave state provision, accountable via elected politicians to the people paying for and receiving it. On the other hand was the Nicholas Ridley model, in which, at its logical extreme, state bodies from the MoD to the NHS to local government became contracting organisations in which elected representatives met periodically simply to agree contracts recommended to them by a skeletal staff of lawyers and procurement officers.

Later we will discuss the policies of the New Labour government, focusing on contradictions and spaces it has opened up, often unintentionally, for

142

people seeking to gain democratic control over public resources. It was a government swept into office by overwhelming popular desire to end the policies of Thatcherism. Indeed you could argue it was not John Major that voters rejected in 1997 but the destruction of the welfare state and the growing gulf between rich and poor. These origins, as well as the presence—albeit not for long—of a minority of ministers and advisers in New Labour committed to significant redistribution and publicly provided public services, has been a source of constant tension and inconsistency in policies. The dominant approach, however (driven by Tony Blair), has included encouraging continued contracting out to private companies of the delivery and management of public services. New Labour's twist on this has been to induce parts of the public sector, for example social housing, to become private 'not for profit' companies in which 'the community' is represented. But these companies, like all companies, are limited by financial markets and commercial law, which limit their ability to be responsive to social need or accountable to the community. Constrained by unreformed commercial company law, 'not for profit' companies represent no new mechanism for providing public goods.

Contracting out *plays* with the idea of a third, organisational, dimension but does not actually practise different principles from those of the state or the market. Indeed, this combination of centrally imposed targets and deference to private companies seems to combine the worst of both worlds. Perhaps one of the difficulties for the government in coming up with a convincing strategy of public service reform is that it has spurned, or been blind to, innovative traditions in the democratising of public administration. Instead, it has treated business as the primary model of administrative efficiency from which the public sector must learn.

'Outside facts'

The growth of the state

Throughout the middle of the twentieth century, state institutions came to carry out functions which, as Keynes put it, 'fall outside the sphere of the individual'. These included control of the supply of money (in an attempt to even out the ups and downs of the capitalist market and keep the resources of the economy fully employed) and provision of public goods and infrastructure (from hospitals and parks, to railways and postal services), so that public spending could meet needs not adequately answered through individuals buying and selling on the market. Further functions assumed by the state included legislation and taxation requiring private companies to behave responsibly towards the rest of society. Behind all these institutions were ethically based economic principles distinct from the market: the allocation of resources according to need, rather than price and ability to pay, financed through redistributive mechanisms including cross-subsidy, progressive taxation and national insurance. The creation of new state institutions and public corporations based on these principles was speeded up by a war against fascism for which the people were willingly mobilised or mobilised themselves.

The 'people's war' created widespread, deeply rooted confidence in the possibilities of mobilising public resources for the common good. The peace-time legacy of this, even 40 years on, made it hard for Mrs Thatcher et al. to stamp out public commitment to public service. But the peculiarities of wartime had established a template of *how* public resources were matched to social need, and there was never any clear break from the wartime framework of simple, singular goals. Thus complexity, change and growing expectations were not built into the structure of the welfare state. Its original decision making structures were based on a highly abstract notion of the universal, in which general principles laid down by elected politicians and implemented in a standardised way seemed sufficient. This was most apparent in public housing which only in the late 1960s began to take account of variety and diversity in housing need. Recognition that the universal can only be manifest concretely and idiosyncratically came later—with feminism, for instance—as 'benevolent' paternalist welfare state assumptions began to be challenged.

For the wartime welfare state, ends justified means—it was all but unconscious of questions of process. Military-type hierarchies were replicated across the public sector, often staffed initially by military personnel.

The parallel growth of corporate power

Facts concerning the dynamic nature of the private market are also relevant. After the Second World War, while the state intervened in the private sector, private business got a grip on the state. 'When the state extends its control over big business, big business moves in to control the state', warned Nye Bevan as early as 1944.[2] Neither the Labour party nor the unions used their members' inside knowledge of industry to counter private industry's effective capture of key sections of the state apparatus (most notably the department of trade and industry but also, from an industry specific perspective, the pharmaceuticals industry's capture of health, the road haulage and car industry's of transport, and the waste industry's of the Department of the Environment. Corporate financial interests held a strong hold over the British state via the Treasury.[3] Although Nye Bevan was characteristically canny enough to alert the labour movement to this, the long-term danger it posed to the social democratic state was not apparent. In the boom conditions of those days the mixed economy appeared stable. But as the boom gave way to tighter markets and a more competitive global economy, mergers, acquisition and rationalisations took place across the private sector on a global scale, causing a dramatic shift in the balance of power between private corporations and the state.

The 1970s saw the emergence of transnational corporations with budgets that matched those of medium sized nations.[4] This meant greater mobility of capital: companies had a wider choice of where to invest. It meant financial markets which were increasingly speculative. Britain was particularly vulnerable to these changes because British capitalism, unlike in say postwar Germany or Scandinavia, had never developed powerful institutions in which the private sector, including the banks, regularly negotiated with the state and the trades unions. Such linking institutions might have protected British social democratic state institutions to some degree from the most socially destructive pressures of global financial markets.[5]

The lack of checks on global corporate forces led to an asymmetry and instability in the Keynesian 'mixed economy' where, as he had conceived it, a public sphere of economic activity would coexist stably with a private sphere. Keynes was optimistic about the joint stock company, thinking it would become more and more like a public corporation. Where the industry concerned, for example the railways, had a strong obligation to serve society, nationalisation would become almost irrelevant, he thought, because the corporation(s) that dominated the industry would already in effect be acting like a public corporation. Although companies publicly quoted on the stock exchange are in many ways different from companies owned by private individuals, they are still driven by the competitive, profit maximising, capital accumulating process. Profits and dividends, especially on British financial markets, remain *the* indicator of success which holds the key to confidence in the company and hence its stability and ability to borrow and expand. As markets become dominated by smaller and smaller numbers of larger and larger companies, pressure intensifies and with it the search for new markets. By the late 1970s, as traditional markets became saturated, they began to look longingly at the public sector which, driven by very different imperatives, was in no position to compete with the private sector on the strictly commercial terms that the Conservative government imposed. What's more, corporations put huge resources into lobbying to open up the public sector to the market. As the government responded to their pressures the Keynesian mixed economy began to change beyond all recognition.

This did not make national governments irrelevant but it led them to serve the needs of global markets. This growth in the power of market-driven institutions also laid the foundation for an increasingly unbounded international market. There was a political dimension to this: governments acquiesced to the lobbying and round tables of leading corporations' pressures. The triumphant way in which free-market politicians seized the symbolic moment of the fall of the Berlin wall and made it theirs when ideologically it could just as well have been social democracy's, led social democratic leaders to act as if the wall had somehow fallen on them. Taken by surprise and without a coherent programme for extending democracy to the administration of state institutions, the social democracies let the fall of the wall annihilate the ideal of public intervention through democratically controlled state institutions.

The erosion of public services

So it was that no sooner had the social democratic state extended its activities, and its notion of citizenship, to include social and economic rights (as well as civic and political rights) than an economic dynamic began that significantly undermined this expansion of rights. This process came to fruition in the late 1970s and most virulently through the 1980s and 90s.

Labour left office in 1979 in confusion, torn between its historic commitments to labour and its inability to bargain effectively with capital. Mrs Thatcher then embarked on deregulation to attract mobile capital to Britain. Mobile capital meant companies on the lookout for new markets, new spheres of investment. One such sphere was the conversion of previously non-market areas—including services—into commodities. Steadily and stealthily, through intense lobbying, strategic alliances and political influence rules were changed and laws passed which opened up local government, the railways, health and education to the private market. Compulsory competitive tendering, subcontracting of ancillary services, the breaking up of services into parts that can be sold at a price, the demoralising and fragmenting transferral of workforces accustomed to providing a public service into companies requiring them to work for profit—all of these processes eroded the foundations of the social democratic state, which had been by definition a body of non-market institutions intended to meet social needs according to democratic principles of organisation and resource allocation.

The new terrain of struggle over the state

New Labour has not reversed the shift from state to market but it has altered the ideological and political terrain in which it takes place. First, seeking to remedy the worst injustices of the Thatcher years, it created openings, albeit ambiguous, for alternative directions within the public sector. The wider political context has not been favourable to these fragile experiments but they provide results from which we can learn. Second, through its continuation of contracting out, New Labour has inadvertently politicised *implementation* (of policies) and *management* within the public sector, stimulating amongst public service trades unions (who assumed Labour was elected to rebuild and extend the sector) new strategies which move beyond protest to the formulation of alternative proposals for public service provision.

Community and democracy

Unlike Thatcher's, New Labour policies express a commitment to society, at least rhetorically. They evoke the concept of 'community' in relation to public services but they posit this notion as an alternative to the state, at times quite explicitly. Alan Whitehead, a former Labour minister for local government, described how 'There was a view that communities are good things; they could tell you what was needed and administrators would go and carry it out without the intermediate layers of political democracy.' A particularly bold and now quietly marginalised government initiative, New Deal for Communities (NDC), illustrates the contradictions in New Labour's relationship to 'the community' and shows people attempting to reroute a government initiative towards democratising state institutions.

NDC's commitment in 1989 was to grant 39 of England's poorest housing estates (of between 3,000 and 11,000 residents per estate) £50 million for each estate for a ten year programme of regeneration. The condition of the funding and the criteria for choosing the estates was that the decisions about the £50 million should be 'community led'. This led to a variety of experiments, some 'community led' only in name, some led by communities too divided or beleaguered to arrive at a sustainable decision-making process, and some where community representatives eventually negotiated a viable structure for genuinely participative democratic institutions. In these cases, local residents briefly had real power over resources and their allocation—conventional forms of representative democracy were strengthened by a new participatory arm, responsive to the needs of the people. In particular, in some NDCs residents' representatives called officials to account and influenced the day to day implementation of policy. In these localities, people ignored the wall put up by the government between community and politics, and expanded the narrow participation rights extended to them to encompass bigger political decisions about the future of services—whether housing, leisure facilities or the role of the local council in regeneration.[6] However, the absence of a framework of radical constitutional reform for local government has meant that the lessons from such innovations in public administration have not been generalised and sometimes faced hostility or even sabotage from parts of local government.

Democracy and public service management

I talked earlier about the erosion of public services, but 'eroded' is the wrong word, implying a gradual organic process rather than an effective dismantlement, involving conflict, power, levers of change and possibilities of reversal or new directions. What has happened since Mrs Thatcher is a radical shift in the centres of power in public sector decision making.

Take local government, for example (though the same process has been going on other services). In the past, the centre of power for key budget decisions was the finance department. Now, an equally important centre of power is the procurement process, led by senior officers in different departments who determine the specifications for tenders. Since every service must now go out to tender, the process of procuring contracts, as much as the amount of money allocated, vitally influences that service.

To resist privatisation, trades unions have opened up this procurement process, in particular putting forward public sector bids for delivery. To this

end, workers, users, committed managers and sometimes councils have
scrutinised the organisation of services from the standpoint of effectiveness
to the public and the use of public money, comparing their results with the
proposals from private companies. I witnessed a very interesting case of this
kind on Tyneside where senior council executives were putting out to contract
'Information Technology and Related Services' (the strategic technical heart of
the council's operations). The assumption was that British Telecom would win
this multimillion contract. The unions were not happy. They insisted that the
council itself put in a bid and they committed themselves to working with
management to produce it. The process of preparing the bid was innovative.
Using a combination of industrial militancy and well researched argument the
unions convinced management to hold day-long sessions with staff, where IT
workers contributed ideas about how the council's IT work could be better
organised to make use of their skills, improve the quality of the service to the
public and even to expand and improve services across the city. The end result
was a bid which managers and councillors agreed was in the better long-term
interests of the city. BT's bid had been attractive because they were offering
immediate investment money to a council in financial crisis. After the unions'
construction of an alternative, however, it was clear that given the profits BT
would cream off and remove, the 'in house' option was economically as well
as socially preferable.

It might be argued that that this democratisation and improvement in the
organisation of the public sector required the marketisation of the public
sector, if not its privatisation. It is true that service provision did need
modernisation. On Tyneside the stimulus came from marketisation and the
consequent threat of privatisation. The responses—processes of positive
trades union involvement and a shift in the balance of power which granted
staff a real say in service delivery—were triggered by the procurement
process. But they could just as well, and more constructively, have been
triggered by a political commitment to democratising local government
administration and management.

An example of that would be in London in the 1980s. Labour's manifesto
for London in 1982 was committed to democratising local government
hierarchy, and under Ken Livingstone the baroque hierarchies of the GLC
were indeed transformed, as was the relation of County Hall to the citizens of
London. Lasting commitment to breaking down such hierarchies and opening
up local government requires a deeper democratisation of local government
itself, through the introduction of proportional representation. This would
put a pressure on politicians to make services responsive to the changing
needs of voters, utilising public service workers' skills and imagination. I will
argue later on that marketisation, inevitably meaning public funding of
private companies to deliver public services, amounts to a weakening of
democratic control. Private contracts are monitored merely through the
formal mechanism of a legal contract when what are needed are deeper
forms of active democracy.[7]

Democracy and choice

New Labour has strangely misread public opinion, over-estimating sympathy for Thatcherite individualism. Thatcherism benefited from a reaction against what was presented as the extremes of collective power in the unions or in local government, but even before Labour was elected surveys showed a public opinion settled into majority stances: wanting public delivery of public services, preferring unions as against no unions, and accepting progressive taxation.[8] Thatcherite individualism certainly had an impact on the popular psyche—it wiped out the final traces of automatic deference to authority. What people took from it, paradoxically, was not a belief in the virtues of the market but a strong sense of individual rights in the face of authority, a rejection of political patronisation or presumption by public officials to know what is good for us.

New Labour's misreading of Thatcherism has led it to adopt a supermarket model of politics and talk of 'consumer choice'. The Office of Public Service Reforms calls public sector users 'customers': it aims to 'improve current structures, systems, incentives and skills to deliver better, more customer-focused services'. This is not just a matter of language. It is about the ideal of the relationships envisaged between individuals and services. Emphasis is on choice of schools, hospitals—even train services and electricity and gas companies—rather than democratic control, as the criterion of quality. Hence 'market research' and 'customer feedback' surveys and consultations are the driving forces of reform, not popular participation in decision making or opening up of the processes of public administration. The picture which Tony Blair generally paints is of a choice for the public sector between emulating the private sector's relationship to the people (as individual consumers taking isolated choices, pursuing individual preferences) or being an old-style bureaucrat, unresponsive to its citizens, endlessly fending them off and passing the buck. The idea of collective action, deliberation, association—that is, a deeper democracy than the ballot box—being built into state structures as an internal force for change is alien to New Labour. Yet people pursue such actions to achieve the services they want. For example, education academic Sally Tomlinson shows that in education the overwhelming demand from parents is not for individual choice but for a good local school. Parents have come together to press for this. In Dulwich, South London, children travelled to 40 different secondary schools, and local parents—oversaturated with 'choice'—formed an association to demand a new local comprehensive.[9] The overwhelming rejection by parents in the early 1990s of the Tory offer for schools to 'opt out' and become grant maintained was an expression of the same preference—for a public service that users and would-be users could influence through social association with each other and involvement in the school's decision making. One feature of the Tory 'opt out' process which particularly annoyed people was the narrowness of the voting constituency. True to its belief that there was no such thing as society, the Thatcherite assumption was that only those with children at the school had any concern for the future of the school.

Ironically, just as New Labour was adopting this model of individual consumerism, consumers began to organise themselves, especially via new internet opportunities for time efficient collectivism, to apply moral and social pressure to corporate policies on labour and the environment.[10] There was a new interest in third dimension questions: how to achieve effective social control over investment; how to use public purchasing to influence corporate policy; how to strengthen the alternative social sector not simply in the subordinate interstices of the corporate economy, but in direct challenge to its heights.

Making democracy powerful

My own feelings are grounded in the social democratic belief that there are basic needs the market cannot meet, based as it is on price and ability to pay. Further, that the meeting of these needs is the responsibility of society as a whole through arrangements democratically agreed. The institutions which represent society at different levels are the elected parliaments, councils and assemblies responsible for state administration funded by the taxpayer. Clearly then the framework of an elected government responsible for allocating and administering public resources is fundamental to the meeting of basic social needs from housing, health, education and protection against destitution, through to security and protection against crime. But what has also become clear in the past twenty years of dismantling the state is that it matters considerably *how* these resources are managed. This is something like a child who almost destroys a toy or piece of household equipment to see what is inside or how it works; we have unwillingly witnessed the dismantling of the welfare state and now in the process of trying to rebuild it we understand more clearly how it should work.

The new forms of democracy that have taken root in the ambiguous spaces opened up under New Labour indicate the possibilities for a genuinely experimental approach to organising public administration. The experiences of community led regeneration show the importance for public employees of structures of accountability as well as of the ability to cooperate with residents' representatives in the implementation of policy in a transparent and rule-governed fashion. Each of these makes public employees into genuinely public servants in the day-to-day sense of 'serving the public'. The experiences of opening up the public procurement process point to the importance for public decision making of means by which public employees can influence the character or style of services and delivery. Public rejection of the consumer choice route to improving service quality suggests that collective deliberation and decision making are what is important when it comes to the expression of diverse individual needs and their fulfilment. Collectively derived decisions can produce better quality solutions than anything imposed from above.

The difference between these and other means of popular control over public resources on the one hand, and the government's deference to the private sector model of efficiency on the other, hinges on understandings of democracy. The government relies heavily on contracts between public officials and private companies as mechanisms of democratic control, but legal contracts are not a sufficient basis for democracy. They are blunt instruments of democracy at best. Many aspects of high quality service cannot be legally summarised—the comfort of continuity of care, for example, or the inner refreshment of a beautiful park, or the creative benefits of a local library where staff welcome and stimulate children's eagerness to browse. Lawyers may delete such references as difficult to codify let alone make legally binding. What is codifiable is attendance or user figures, but since there may be no alternative provision these cannot measure satisfaction. Moreover, genuine democratic control by users as well as politicians requires open access to information—access that most private companies refuse to give on the grounds of 'commercial confidentiality'.

Where can the impetus come from to develop a service to meet the changing needs of communities? In theory, market competition is a source of innovation. But the relationship of public service deliverers to their clients is not a simple market–customers relationship. And the big corporations now contracted to deliver our social services face no serious competition. Having locked the local authority or hospital or government department into a contract, they will be costly to dismiss. The legal contract may speak of consultation, but consultation via what mechanisms? Market research methods—focus groups and surveys—are inadequate means of engaging people's creativity.

If, as almost every senior public official admits, handing management over to a private company means cutting the wage bill, where is the will, realistically, to harness the insights and skills of stressed and demoralised front line workers? This is not an argument for going back to the organisation of the state as it used to be— traditional methods of public management have also failed to release the creativity of their workforce, stifling, for instance, ideas for improvements. In fact, the almost army-like hierarchies we described earlier—mirrored by the defensive character of much public sector trade unionism—has meant the squandering of one of the public sector's greatest resources—its workers' knowledge.

As it grew, without any commensurate strengthening or deepening of mechanisms of democratic control, cracks appeared between the people and the policies they voted for and the supposedly public institutions for implementing these policies. Into these cracks anti-democratic interests had insinuated themselves, whether through powerful private lobbies or bureaucratic empires.

New mentalities, new processes

The answer is not a return to 1945, nor is it to replace institutions of public administration with private companies who pursue profit, seeking to cut costs to make them 'efficient' in money terms. Public service has different notions of 'efficiency' which concern social needs that the market does not measure. 'Value for money' cannot be measured by legally definable targets. It requires constant evaluation in which service users have some real power. The thinness of representative democracy needs to be enriched by more direct public involvement in the implementation of policy. The priority then is to address and remedy the weakness of electoral forms of democratic control, 'representative democracy', over the state apparatus. The problem is to find ways of making responsive mechanisms to transmit the needs of the service users to service designers and deliverers.

This enrichment is partly a matter of new institutional thinking, drawing where possible from innovations in practice and therefore likely to have a measure of the new terrain. But it is also a matter of the methodology, culture and mentality that dominates government and politics. Two statements, one by Tom Paine and the other by Beatrice Webb, show contrasting assumptions that can underlie public policy. Each has fundamentally different implications for the nature of public institutions—that is, in the language I adopted at the beginning, for the nature of the third dimension.

Beatrice Webb, a powerful influence on the welfare state, summed up the orthodoxy that underpinned it thus: 'We have little faith in the "average sensual man". We do not believe that he can do much more than describe his grievances, we do not think he can prescribe his remedies.' The assumption here is that the knowledge relevant to social change was exclusively scientific and statistical—available only to the trained mind of the state official, academic expert or professional politician. Other forms of knowledge—as expressed, for example, in the daily lives of people without institutional power—were just 'common sense', superstition, emotion or whatever and irrelevant to public policy. Contrast Webb's words with Tom Paine's in *The Rights of Man*:

It appears to general observation, that revolutions create genius and talent; but those events do no more than bring them forward. There is existing in man, a mass of sense lying in a dormant state, and which unless something excites it to action, will descend with him, in that condition, to the grave. As it is to the advantage of society that the whole of its facilities should be employed, the construction of government ought to be such as to bring forward, by quiet and regular operation, all that capacity which never fails to appear in revolution.

Paine's approach accords with what we now call tacit knowledge—that is, practical and other forms of non-codified, non-science-based knowledge. State institutions lag behind the revolutions that have taken place in our understandings of knowledge, however, which is one reason why social democratic institutions were vulnerable to the extreme individualism of the reaction against the state institutions of the Soviet bloc, with their claims to know and predict the needs of the people. There are two crucial implications of Paine's words. First; practical knowledge and skill can be shared and socialised—becoming a resource for democratic, participatory decision making. Second, radical participatory democracy is coupled to the social efficiency of government. All too often 'participation' is an add-on—at best moralistic and politically correct, at worst a cynical PR ploy. By grounding his ideas of government in an understanding of human capacity, Paine argues for government institutions designed, from their foundations, to bring such capacities forward.

There is no one form that the regular and quiet operations of such a genuinely capacity building and utilising process need take. Indeed, the devising of such forms would be a pilot deployment of the capacities they hope to foster. We can draw out some vital principles from experiments to support this suggestion

My earlier UK examples illustrate the importance of popular participation in the community and the workplace, and possible forms for participation. They indicate ways of strengthening the power of popular control by building democratic pressures into policy implementation processes. They show us participatory democracy surviving precariously in the crevices of the existing power structure, able to relate only to the micro-level of state institutions with very little purchase on national politics, though with an echo and parallels internationally.

Democratic bargaining power: the role of participatory democracy

It is possible to draw further principles from more ambitious, politically committed attempts to develop participatory democratic institutions. The participatory budgeting initiated through the Workers Party (PT) in Brazil provides a well established example of an institutionally embedded and rules-governed process.[11] In an open and transparent process of negotiation local residents can participate directly, through a combination of open plenaries and elected recallable delegates, in deciding the priorities for new investments city wide. In Porto Alegre, for example, through fifteen years of trial and error a well elaborated set of institutions has been developed through which citizens participate in setting public spending priorities for their neighbourhood and city. Delegates of participatory budget processes then negotiate with the mayor and the city councillors.

A key principle here is politicians sharing power. As the late Celso Daniel, a former mayor of Santo André, another 'participatory' city, put it: 'We believed in taking the principles of democracy from social movements, including the trade union movement, with us when we gained office. That meant we had to share political power, the management of the city with the community.'

Power sharing means the coexistence and mutual negotiation between two sets of democratic institutions, two sources of democratic legitimacy—one representative, one participative.

Representative democracy's legitimacy stems from the minimal but equal participation of all through the vote, whereas the legitimacy of participatory democracy lies in the high degree of activity of what is likely to be a minority through institutions that are transparent, open to all and based on mutually agreed rules. Representative institutions determine the principles and general direction of an elected government. The processes of participatory democracy provide ways in which the people can play a further decisive role in the detailed elaboration of these principles. The open, rule-governed process of popular participation in proposing the detailed priorities of a budget, for example, or managing a local public facility, has more democratic legitimacy than a group of officials working behind closed doors, often doing their own deals with certain social groups and economic interests. Participatory democracy also plays a vital role in monitoring the work of the executive and state apparatus, able to go where and know what politicians cannot.

Participatory institutions generate self-confident expectations which lead to pressure—in the form of lobbying or campaigning—being applied to the representative elected bodies. Formally, representative democracy has the final say, but since representatives must seek re-election in a multiparty system, then—as long as the electoral system is fair and democratic—they have to be responsive to proposals drawn up by their constituents.

The experience of Brazilian cities like Porto Alegre and Santo André bear out the Paine link between social efficiency ('it is to the advantage of society that the whole of its faculties be employed') and democracy ('the construction of government ought . . . to bring forward all that capacity'). First, participatory processes close the gaps between elections and the work of state institutions, into which corruption, vested interests and empire building can creep (before the participatory budget corruption was rife; now it is rare). Second, participatory processes, involving as they do a high proportion of poorer citizens, have redistributed wealth and resources to poorer communities. This was part of the PT's mandate but it went against many vested interests and would probably not have been achieved without the additional lever of power which the participatory process gave to the poor, those who stood to gain from the PT election. Third, participation has led to higher quality services partly because its power is not simply to set priorities but also to monitor the implementation of these priorities. Finally, the new system of managing public resources through a combination of electoral and participative democracy means an overall gain in democratic legitimacy and as a result, potentially, in democratic power. People are more likely to feel like, in Tom Paine's terms, 'proprietors in government'. This sense of popular ownership has itself been a source of bargaining power with private corporations wishing to locate in the city. There are several examples in Porto Alegre, for instance, of multinational retailers wanting to build supermarkets and having to enter a hard bargaining process stimulated by the participatory budget, leading to significant social gains such as the company creating extra jobs, or providing training and extra space for local shops at affordable rents. Participation-enhanced democratic power has been a source of strength in bargaining with international bodies like the World Bank too.

These are not neat, finished institutions, models for a new kind of state. They are not spontaneous outbursts of rebellion either, as participatory democracy is sometimes caricatured. Rather, they are lasting sources of democratic bargaining power with private and public institutions otherwise beyond the reach of the people involved in the participatory process. We could call participatory democracy an 'embedded' source of democratic bargaining power; as well as the internal impact of democratising the management of public resources, there is an external benefit—the strengthening of local democracy when bargaining with outside bodies that influence citizens' lives.

This idea challenges the traditional liberal division between politics and economics. 'Embedded' bargaining power provides political institutions with a means of standing up to the anti-democratic pressures of private corporations; it also points to ways in which political institutions can ally with economic pressures for democracy. Alliances with cooperatives, the social economy generally, with trades unions and others working for democratic control over pension funds, with consumer campaigns against corporate injustices—all these contribute to wider economic democracy, without which participatory democracy will remain always unfinished and under threat.

This notion of embedded bargaining power implies the possibility—and necessity—of reforming the state through a process of democratisation and stimulating in civil society sources of countervailing democratic power to both the state and private capital. This is not to say that the two processes are necessarily and always compatible or without tension. They contain different logics: the actual reform of the state takes place within an institutional framework of representative democracy, whereas the building of counter-power involves an open ended process of experiment with new untested sources of democratic power. But in their different ways the experiences of Newcastle and Porto Alegre illustrate that this process of building counter-power, messy and uneven as it can be, provides a kick start and a source of continuing energy for reforming the state. It is necessary to reinforce the ability of elected representatives to carry through the will of the people in the face of obstacles presented from within the state bureaucracy and the private market. This way of seeing institutions in terms of bargaining power recognises democracy as a constant struggle, never an end state.

The case of Brazil, where Luiz Inacio 'Lula' da Silva, leader of the Workers Party, was elected President with a 68% vote, presents us starkly with the most difficult challenge for democratic bargaining power: how to counter the power of financial markets, the IMF and the US Treasury. Together, these unelected financial forces are pressing the Brazilian government to repay debts—including debts accumulated under the dictatorship—at a level that is destroying Lula's ability to carry out his mandate. The Brazilian dilemma is a further confirmation that no longer can strategies for a democratising the state be a matter merely of designing new institutions of democratic administration. They have also to maximise democratic power in the face of extra-democratic threats. Not only local and national sources of democratic pressure and reinforcement are needed, but also the growing international movements for democracy, evident since the Seattle protests against the World Trade Organisation, and on the streets again in growing numbers against Bush's and Blair's war against Iraq.

Democracy is not inevitable. Forms of reaction and authoritarianism are as I write, in spring 2004, powerful on the world scene. But just as Keynes described an underlying move towards state intervention where markets failed, now we can sketch the ways in which people are inventing stronger forms of democracy where earlier forms have lost their vigour. The more we understand such a dynamic, the better able we are to seize opportunities to assist its progress.

Acknowledgements

My thanks to Hilary Bichovsky, Mark Cresswell and Joyce Wainwright.

Notes

1 See Robin Blackburn, *Banking on Death or Investing in Death? The History and Future of Pensions*, London, Verso, 2003.
2 Labour Party Conference Report, 1944.
3 See Geoffrey Ingham, *The Nature of Money*, Cambridge, Polity Press, 2004.
4 Richard J. Barnett, *Global Reach: The Power of the Multinational Corporations*, New York, Simon and Schuster, 1974.
5 Colin Leys, *Market Driven Politics: Neoliberal Democracy and the Public Interest*, London, Verso, 2001.
6 See Hilary Wainwright, *Reclaim the State: Experiments in Popular Democracy*, London, Verso, 2003.
7 See Angela Eagle, *A Deeper Democracy: Challenging Market Fundamentalism*, Catalyst Working Paper, London, Catalyst, 2003.
8 For example, Roger Jowell et al., *British Social Attitudes: The 14th Report—the End of Conservative Values?*, National Centre for Social Research, 1997.
9 Quoted in Catherine Needham, *Citizen-Consumers: New Labour's Market-place Democracy*, Catalyst Working Paper, London, Catalyst, 2003.
10 See the 'boycotts list' held by *Ethical Consumer*: http://www.ethicalconsumer.org/boycotts_list.htm
11 Hilary Wainwright, *Reclaim the State*, pp. 42–69.

Index

accountability 57, 93, 94, 120, 121, 132–3
Adam Smith Institute 24
Amnesty International 53
Anderson, Perry 24
anti-statism 12
Asquith, H. H. 25
associational economy 106, 108
audit society 59, 60, 69–70
Australia 137

Bank of England 65
Bastiat, Frederic 12, 20
BBC World Service 53
Bell Laboratories 74
Bevan, Nye 144
Birmingham City Council 95, 126
Blair, Tony 58, 59–60, 61–2, 71, 141, 143, 149, 156
Blears, Hazel 123
Blunkett, David 69, 117
Bobbitt, P. 24, 52
Brazil 153, 154–6
Bright, J. 24
British Telecom 148
Brittan, S. 24, 29
Brown, Gordon 6–7, 7, 93
Buchanan, J. 24, 30
bureaucracy 29–31
Bush, George W. 141, 156
business
    motives and functions 77–9
    legitimacy of power 76

Cabinet Office 71, 137–8
Camden Borough Council 127
Campbell, Alastair 58, 59
Canada 44–5, 119, 137
centralisation 91–2
    and marketisation 57–60
    strong state 102–4
centralism 8, 102
    reformed 94
Cerny, Philip G. 39–49
Chile 15
China 79–80

Churchill, Winston 58
citizenship 5, 121, 122
civil servants , 58–9, 60, 69, 70–1
civil service 59, 69, 135
Clinton, Bill 58
Cobden, R. 24
Cole, G. D. H. 2, 61
Cologne 112–13
Common Agricultural Policy 20
community 106, 108
Compagnie General des Eaux 74
competition state 40–9
Conservative government 2–3
coordination 133–4
    in decentred state 136–7
corporate hierarchy 107–8, 109–11
corporate power 76, 144–5
Crosland, C. A. R. 16, 34–5, 52, 61

Daniel, Celso 153
Darwinism 82
da Silva, Luiz Inacio 155–6
decentralisation 5, 130–9
    see also new localism
de Jasay, A. 24
democratisation of public services 147–8
    see also new localism
democracy
    and choice 149–50
    and community 146–7
    and public service management 147–8
direct democracy 20–1
distributive justice 25–6, 27–9
Dulwich 149
Dunn, John 67
Durbin, Evan 52, 61

eBay 92
education 4, 13, 16, 89–90, 92, 149–50
    see also higher education
Elizabeth I, Queen 52
employment contracts 109, 110
Enron 77, 85, 110
equality 7, 16
    of opportunity 26

Published by Blackwell Publishing Ltd, 9600 Garsington Road, Oxford OX4 2DQ, UK and 350 Main Street, Malden, MA 02148, USA

The

Political Quarterly

Founded in 1930

EDITORS
Andrew Gamble and **Tony Wright**

LITERARY EDITOR
Donald Sassoon

REPORTS AND SURVEYS EDITOR
Jean Seaton

Assistant Editor: Stephen Ball

Information for subscribers
The Political Quarterly is published four times a year, in January, April, July and October (with a fifth issue in book form which is included in the subscription costs), by Blackwell Publishing, 9600 Garsington Road, Oxford OX4 2DQ or 350 Main Street, Malden, MA 02148. Back issues are available from the publisher. New orders and sample copy requests should be addressed to the Journals Marketing Manager at the publisher's address above (or by email to jnlsamples@blackwellpublishers.co.uk, quoting the name of the journal). Renewals, claims and all other correspondence relating to subscriptions should be addressed to Blackwell Publishing Journals, PO Box 1354, 9600 Garsington Road, Oxford OX4 2DQ, UK (tel: +44(0)1865 778315, fax: +44(0)1865 471775 or email: customerservices@oxon.blackwellpublishing.com). Cheques should be made payable to Blackwell Publishing Ltd. All subscriptions are supplied on a calendar year basis.

Subscription Prices 2004	Europe (Euro zone)	The Americas	UK and Rest of World
Institutions	£148.00	US$282.00	£174.00
Individuals (UK only)	€35.00	US$37.00	£23.00